Research Reports on College Transitions | No. 2

2009 National Survey of First-Year Seminars:
Ongoing Efforts to Support Students in Transition

Ryan D. Padgett & Jennifer R. Keup

Cite as:

Padgett, R. D., & Keup, J. R. (2011). *2009 National Survey of First-Year Seminars: Ongoing efforts to support students in transition* (Research Reports on College Transitions No. 2). Columbia, SC: University of South Carolina, National Resource Center for The First-Year Experience and Students in Transition.

Production Staff for the National Resource Center:
Project Editor   Toni Vakos, Editor
Design and Production   Shana Bertetto, Graphic Artist

Cover image provided by USC Creative Services

Library of Congress Cataloging-in-Publication Data

Padgett, Ryan D.
  2009 national survey of first-year seminars : ongoing efforts to support students in transition / Ryan D. Padgett, Jennifer R. Keup.
      p. cm. -- (Research reports on college transitions ; No. 2)
  Includes bibliographical references and index.
  ISBN 978-1-889271-80-4 (alk. paper)
  1. College student orientation--United States--Evaluation. 2. Educational surveys--United States. I. Keup, Jennifer R. II. Title.
  LB2343.32.P33 2011
  378.1'980973--dc23
                    2011037219

The authors would like to acknowledge and thank Cindy A. Kilgo and Helen Mulhern Halasz for their critical perspectives and analytical contributions to this research brief.

Contents

List of Figures and Tables

Figures

Tables

Introduction

Far from a recent innovation, first-year seminars have roots dating from the late 19th century. While there is some debate with respect to the exact date of origin for these curricular interventions, evidence of first-year seminars can be found as early as the 1880s (Barefoot & Fidler, 1996; Fitts & Swift, 1928). Much like today, early examples of these courses addressed different student adjustment needs, including general orientation (e.g., Boston University in 1888); introduction to a specific major (e.g., freshman lecture series offered in the mechanical engineering department at the University of Michigan in 1900; career exploration (e.g., Oberlin College in 1900); or specific academic topics as with "Dartmouth College's course entitled 'Evolution' [and] Columbia College's course, begun in 1924,...entitled 'Introduction to Contemporary Civilization'" (Gordon, 1989, p. 187). Further, most of these early seminars were typically elective and not offered for credit (Gordon). The first seminar to be integrated to the first-year curriculum for credit was at Reed College in 1911 (Fitts & Swift) and focused on "the purpose of college, the college curriculum, the individual plan of study, student honesty, student government, intercollegiate athletics, and college religion" (Gordon, p. 185).

Several forces in the early 1900s led a number of institutions across the country to adopt first-year orientation courses. The expectations of in loco parentis at that time demanded that institutions look for ways to address students' social, personal, and academic adjustment and well-being in their transition to college (Saunders & Romm, 2008). Further, the sizable increase in the number of college students after World War I and the rapid evolution of student personnel services at that time caused institutions to seek ways to address the holistic adjustment needs of a large number of students (Cohen & Kisker, 2010; Gordon, 1989; Sandeen & Barr, 2006). First-year seminars became a flexible tool to meet these demands efficiently and effectively. By the 1920s and 1930s, nearly 100 American universities, many of them elite institutions, offered first-year seminars and the vast majority of them required the course (Gordon; Koch & Gardner, 2006).

By the late 1930s, the prevalence and scope of first-year seminars on college campuses began to decline, most notably due to faculty objections to their perceptions of the seminar as lacking in academic rigor and collective frustration with the life adjustment content of the course (Caple, 1964; Gordon, 1989). As such, it became challenging to recruit instructors and gain support for the course within the undergraduate curriculum. When combined with the end of in loco parentis, the adoption of an institutional "'sink or swim' attitude toward first-year students" (Gahagan, 2002, p. 5), and the increased importance that the new generation of students placed on peer culture over institutional support structures, first-year seminars slowly lost their foothold in American higher education (Cohen & Kisker, 2010; Gordon; Saunders & Romm, 2008).

In the late 1970s and early 1980s, first-year seminars experienced a resurgence of interest as institutions attempted to address concerns about access, equity, and retention in American higher education (Gahagan, 2002). At that time, colleges and universities "rediscovered first-year seminars as an important tool...to facilitate the success of entering college students and to enhance first-to-second year retention rates among the general population of entering students, particularly among academically underprepared, first-generation, and historically under-represented students" (Keup, 2005-2006, p. 63). While this renaissance of first-year seminars was initially offered as an intervention strategy to serve and support potentially at-risk students, the success of the course has caused it to be more generally applied. Data suggest as many as 94% of participating institutions in a large national survey on the first year of college offer a first-year seminar to all types of new college students (Policy Center on the First Year of College, 2002), and often to serve as the cornerstone of "an intentional combination of academic and co-curricular efforts" (Koch & Gardner, 2006, p. 2) that comprise a first-year experience program.

Studying the First-Year Seminar

Renewed interest in the first-year seminar also led to both assessment and research on its impact on first-year students and their adjustment experiences. Further, the continued maturation of higher education as its own graduate academic discipline during the 1970s and 1980s, the growth in accountability within higher education, and the increase in institutional assessment efforts also contributed to the academic study of first-year seminars and their effect on new students' experiences and success. Several early studies on first-year seminars were released in the scholarly literature in the 1970s and 1980s (Shanley & Witten, 1990). However, they were often limited by the lack of standard operational definitions for first-year seminar, institution-specific samples, and a narrow context in which to understand their structure and use.

In 1988, the first National Survey of First-Year Seminars was administered by the National Resource Center for The First-Year Experience and Students in Transition (then called the National Resource Center for The Freshman Year Experience) and the resulting monograph, published in 1991, "was the first known attempt to provide a national, empirical snapshot of the first-year seminar" (Tobolowsky, 2005, p. 11). Further, in 1992, Barefoot engaged in research for her doctoral dissertation, which "analyzed approximately 500 course descriptions and other related materials" to create a typology that helped standardize the discussion of different types of seminars on college campuses across the country (Tobolowsky, p. 11). Both of these efforts represented the beginning of an ongoing process to collect and analyze national data on first-year seminars toward the creation of a common vocabulary for discussing the characteristics of these courses and a national context in which to interpret institutional decisions and structures for first-year seminars. Those research projects yielded a definition and typology that are still in use today. More specifically, a first-year seminar is

> a course intended to enhance the academic and/or social integration of first-year students by introducing them (a) to a variety of specific topics, which vary by seminar type; (b) to essential skills for college success; and (c) to selected processes, the most common of which is the creation of a peer support group. (Barefoot, p. 49)

Five types of first-year seminars emerged from the analyses of the data collected (Barefoot, 1992) and have been used throughout the survey's history (e.g., Barefoot & Fidler, 1992; Barefoot & Fidler, 1996; Tobolowsky, 2005; Tobolowsky & Associates, 2008), including

◇ *Extended orientation.* These seminars tend to focus on "student survival and success techniques" (Hunter & Linder, 2005, p. 279). Sometimes called freshman orientation, college survival, college transition, or student success courses, the content of these seminars often includes an introduction to campus resources, time management, academic and career planning, learning strategies, and an introduction to student development issues.

◇ *Academic with uniform content across sections.* These seminars have a primary focus on an academic theme or discipline but will often include academic skills components, such as critical thinking and expository writing. This seminar type includes generally uniform academic content across sections, which can be interdisciplinary or theme-oriented and "may sometimes be part of an institution's general education or core curriculum" (Hunter & Linder, p. 279).

◇ *Academic on various topics.* These seminars are similar to academic seminars with uniform content except that specific topics vary from section to section. Often, the courses are "fashioned...on faculty members' individual areas of academic or personal interest and expertise" (Hunter & Linder, p. 280), thereby creating a palate of seminar choices from which students may select.

◇ *Preprofessional or discipline-linked.* Designed to prepare students for the demands of a major or discipline and a profession, these seminars are usually taught within professional schools, specific disciplines, or majors, such as engineering, health sciences, business, law, or education.

◇ *Basic study skills.* These seminars are "generally offered to students lacking appropriate college-level academic skills" (Hunter & Linder, p. 280) and focus on basic academic skills, such as grammar, note taking, test-taking strategies, and critical reading techniques.

Over the years, such discrete categories for first-year seminars became more challenging to use as institutions started to offer more than one type and to blend characteristics of various seminars into one course. As such, the 2006 National Survey for First-Year Seminars introduced a sixth type of seminar called *hybrid* in order to capture those seminars that intentionally blended elements from two or more other types of seminars and place them in their own category of the typology.

The development of this schema and the National Resource Center's efforts to collect a pool of national data proved to be a boon to research on this popular curricular intervention. This has led to the emergence of an extensive literature base describing outcomes related to first-year seminar participation. Indeed, the first-year seminar may be the most researched course in the undergraduate curriculum (summarized in Koch, 2001; Koch, Foote, Hinkle, Keup, & Pistilli, 2007; Pascarella & Terenzini, 2005; Tobolowsky, Cox, & Wagner, 2005). In short, this research has established the first-year seminar as one of the most important instructional vehicles for achieving the learning and developmental objectives of undergraduate education in the United States. Summing up this body of research, Pascarella and Terenzini suggest

> FYS [first-year seminar] participation has statistically significant and substantial, positive effects on a student's successful transition to college and the likelihood of persistence into the second year as well as on academic performance while in college and on a considerable array of other college experiences known to be related directly and indirectly to bachelor's degree completion. (p. 403)

The 2009 National Survey of First-Year Seminars

The 2009 National Survey of First-Year Seminars represents the ninth triennial administration of this survey (survey methodology for the 2009 administration is provided in Appendix A). Much like previous administration cycles, the 2009 Survey asked institutions to provide institutional information and programmatic characteristics of these courses. Content for the 2009 Survey is provided in Appendix B, and general categories of questionnaire items included

◇ Administration of the seminar (e.g., number of sections offered, campus unit administering the seminar, structure of leadership, and oversight for the course)
◇ Seminar characteristics, such as size, duration, credit hours, method of grading, and whether it was required or elective
◇ Number, proportion, and type of students who took the first-year seminar
◇ Professional roles, training opportunities, and compensation for the seminar instructor
◇ Assessment goals, strategies, and outcomes for the first-year seminar

The administration from October 2009 through January 2010 generated responses from 1,019 colleges and universities across the country, which represents a survey response rate of approximately 40% (Appendix C contains a list of institutions responding to the 2009 Survey). Of the more than 1,000 institutional responses, 890 campuses (i.e., 86.5% of the total respondent pool) reported they offered at least one type of first-year seminar to their new students. Given the interest of the National Resource Center on the characteristics and impact of first-year seminars, the 890 colleges and universities with these courses became the sample for the research study reported in this volume.

The administration of the 2009 National Survey was intended to draw a broad sample of institutions, and hundreds of colleges and universities from every institutional type, control, and size responded to the invitation to share data on their first-year seminar. Table 1 shows the distribution of the sample of institutions reporting that they had first-year seminars across several key institutional characteristics. As noted therein, the survey sample overrepresents four-year institutions and larger campuses and shows an overrepresentation of public colleges and universities. Further, this sample includes a greater proportion of more selective institutions and a lower percentage of inclusive and two-year campuses than the national average. These over/underrepresentations of various institutional characteristics may skew the distribution of the types of seminars offered across a national sample. However, these distributions align closely with prior administrations of the survey.

While not nationally representative, this sample does comprise the most comprehensive data set of institutional information on first-year seminars. As such, they provide a national portrait of current practices and structural characteristics for first-year seminars and a national context to inform institutional decisions for these courses. In aggregate, these data offer a broad picture of the current status of these courses and suggest emerging areas and future directions for first-year seminars.

Table 1
Characteristics of Responding Institutions With First-Year Seminars (n = 890)

	Percent of responding institutions with first-year seminars	National percent
Institutional type		
Two-year	26.4	38.3
Four-year	73.6	61.7
Institutional affiliation		
Private	47.9	62.0
Public	52.1	38.0
First-year class size		
500 or less	34.3	49.1
501 - 1,000	23.6	22.4
1,001 - 2,000	19.9	12.9
2,001 -3,000	8.3	6.0
3,001 - 4,000	6.1	3.0
4,001+	7.9	3.1
Institutional selectivity		
Two-year college	26.6	39.7
Special focus institution	5.2	18.5
Inclusive	13.5	18.8
Selective	32.4	15.7
More selective	15.1	7.3

Note. Figures for the national percentages are from *The Integrated Postsecondary Education Data System* at http://nces.ed.gov/IPEDS and *The Carnegie Classification of Institutions of Higher Education* at http://classifications.carnegiefoundation.org/.

The organization of this volume is intended to provide data in a manner that is accessible and informative for higher education researchers and practitioners with varying levels of methodological sophistication and comfort with statistics. The research brief is organized into thematically focused sections, which may be read individually or as a complete volume. In addition, responses to each survey item are analyzed by institutional type (two-year or four-year institution), institutional control (public vs. private), first-year class size (comparable to past analyses of seminar data that used institutional size), and primary type of first-year seminar (as measured by the seminar type with the highest student enrollment). The volume and detail of the overall and disaggregated data points should satisfy the most empirically driven professionals. Discussions of the primary findings of interest, tabular and figurative highlights from in-depth analyses of the aggregate data, and summaries of analyses by subcategories are also provided. This type of data will be of interest to those colleagues who are seeking more summative coverage of the study. While not every statistically significant finding is featured, nearly all major patterns of significant findings are addressed in the narrative. The concluding section brings all of the different areas of analysis and topics together and offers insights and practical implications from the 2009 data.

As a final statement for optimal use of this research brief, it is important to establish a number of guidelines and thresholds used throughout the analyses. As referenced in the detailed description of survey methodology contained in Appendix A, chi-square analyses were conducted to assess whether comparison groups were statistically independent of each other. One limitation to chi-square tests that is of particular interest to the current analyses is the number of observable cases within a comparison group. An assumption within chi-square testing is that the expected cell count is large enough for a chi-square distribution to be applicable to the sample size. Though the common rule within chi-square analysis is to have five or more cases within a cell, a conservative approach was taken within these analyses and the threshold for expected cell size is 10 or more cases. In other words, a statistically significant finding based on a survey response that yielded fewer than 10 cases (and subsequently a low percentage) was interpreted with caution. Though this result is theoretically and statistically significant, there may be little to no practical significance when applied across various institutional controls.

Conclusion

The proffered historical background provides the foundation for the 2009 administration of the National Survey and this current installment in the ongoing research agenda on first-year seminars. It is the authors' hope that the data, interpretations, and conclusions presented in this research brief serve as a valuable tool to faculty, staff, and other seminar leaders in their institutional efforts to ensure the relevance and excellence of these courses as well as validate previous research results and identify new directions of inquiry. Ultimately, first-year seminars have an incredible capacity to facilitate the transition and success of entering students. Any new information, such as the data provided in this research brief, can help higher education professionals realize the full potential of these courses on student experiences and outcomes.

Seminar Types, Characteristics, and Administration

Institutions often take unique approaches to incorporate a seminar that best serves their mission and academic purpose. To uncover the various seminar course types and purposes, this section examines the types of first-year seminars offered, the primary seminar type, student participation in the seminar, student populations required to take a seminar, class size, course objectives, and seminar topics. Statistical evidence is also provided to document how institutions of higher education organize and structure their first-year seminars.

Participation in a First-Year Seminar

The 2009 administration of the National Survey of First-Year Seminars yielded a sample size of 890 institutions (out of 1,019 total respondents) who offered some type of first-year seminar at their college or university. This suggests that 87.3% of survey respondents—representing a national sample of American higher education institutions—offer a first-year seminar, which is consistent with earlier administrations and complements other national data that report 94% of accredited four-year colleges and universities in the United States offer a first-year seminar to at least some students (Policy Center on the First-Year of College, 2002).

The institutions[1] appear to be enrolling a high percentage of students into their first-year seminars. More than two thirds ($n = 618, 70.3\%$) of the institutions report that half of their first-year students participated in a seminar, and over half ($n = 452, 51.4\%$) report that 90% to 100% of their first-year students participated in a seminar. In other words, the overall percentage of first-year students who participated in a first-year seminar at each institution yielded a negatively skewed distribution (Figure 1).

When these data were disaggregated across a number of institutional characteristics, significant disparities emerged among institutional participation rates for first-year seminars. Figure 1 illustrates the percentage of first-year students who take a seminar across two- and four-year institutions. Survey responses indicated that four-year institutions were four times more likely to have their entire first-year student population enrolled in a seminar compared to two-year institutions ($p < 0.01$). Furthermore, 20.5% of two-year institutions reported that *less than 10%* of their first-year students participated in a seminar, while only 3.1% of four-year institutions reported that *less than 10%* participated in a seminar. The percentage of first-year students who participated in a seminar at two-year institutions represents a slight U-shaped distribution, indicating that community colleges tend to enroll a large proportion of students in seminars or very few. Comparatively, the

---

[1] From this point forward, institutions refer to those colleges and universities that report offering a first-year seminar course ($n = 890$).

negatively skewed distribution of four-year institutions highlights the large proportion of students who participate in a seminar; nearly 80% of four-year institutions reported that half or more of their students participated in a seminar.

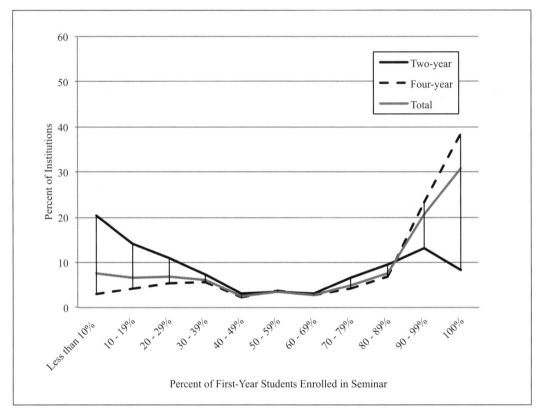

Figure 1. Percentage of students who took a first-year seminar course by institutional type (n = 879).

The distribution of seminar participation across institutional control is similar to that across institutional type. Figure 2 illustrates the percentage of students who took a seminar across public and private institutions, with seminar participation at public institutions represented by a slight U-shaped distribution. Similar to two-year institutions, public institutions were more likely to enroll a large proportion of students in seminars or very few. Conversely, 89.7% of private institutions reported that more than half of their first-year students participated in a seminar, with 52.5% reporting that all first-year students participated in a seminar. Compared to public institutions, private institutions were five times more likely ($p < 0.01$) to offer a seminar to their entire first-year student population (10.5% and 52.5%, respectively).

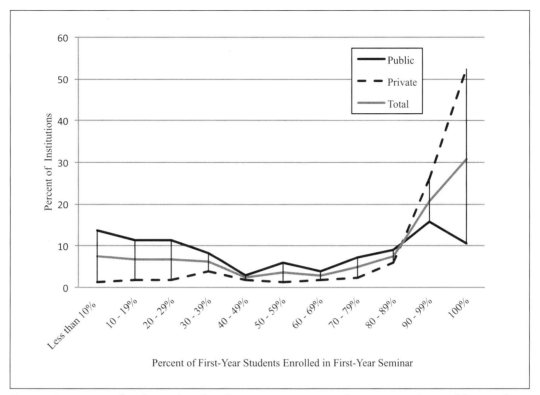

Figure 2. Percentage of students who take a first-year seminar course by institutional control ($n = 879$).

As Figure 3 illustrates, institutions with smaller entering first-year classes[2] had higher percentages of students who participated in a seminar. Institutions with a first-year class of fewer than 500 were eight times more likely than institutions with a first-year class greater than 4,001 to have their entire first-year population participate in a seminar ($p < 0.01$). This suggests that an inverse relationship existed between first-year class size and seminar participation.

---

[2] It is important to note that only a small percentage (7.5%) of institutions that had an entering first-year classes larger than 4,001 participated in the Survey. Accordingly, analyses across institutional size are slightly skewed toward institutions with smaller first-year classes. Further, based on the frequency distribution of respondents, the 10-response set for first-year class size was collapsed to six categories (See Appendix B).

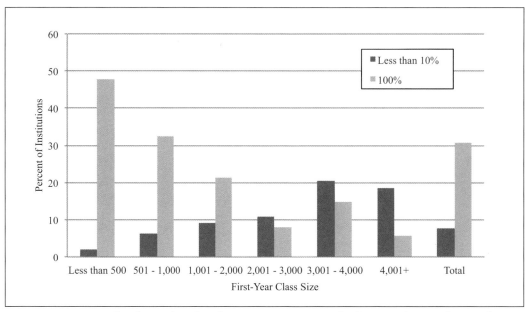

Figure 3. Percentage of students who take a first-year seminar course by first-year class size (*n* = 879).

Types of Seminars Offered

Since its inception, one of the primary components of the National Survey of First-Year Seminars is the identification of seminar type. Initially, five seminar types were recognized: (a) extended orientation, (b) academic with uniform content, (c) academic on various topics, (d) preprofessional or discipline-linked, and (e) basic study skills. In addition, respondents could select *other* for seminars that did not adhere to the five predetermined categories. The 2006 administration introduced a *hybrid* option to better parse out differences between the five seminar types and respondents who selected *other*. For consistency purposes, the 2009 Survey administration adhered to the same categorical selection as the 2006 administration. The introduction in this report provides detailed definitions of the six seminar types. It is important to note that respondents were able to report if their institution offered more than one first-year seminar type, but detailed information about course organization and administration was collected for only the primary seminar (i.e., the type with the highest enrollment) within the institutional setting.

Extended orientation was the most dominant seminar type (61.7%) across all institutions (Figure 4)—a pattern consistent with earlier survey administrations. In fact, institutions offering extended orientation courses were up nearly 4% from 2006 (Tobolowsky & Associates, 2008).[3] This suggests that the majority of institutions use the first-year seminar as a programmatic tool to—as defined in the previous section—introduce students to campus resources, time management skills,

---

[3] It is important to note the survey sample (i.e., institutions) changes with each survey administration. As such, we encourage caution when examining trends across survey administrations for particular seminar characteristics.

academic and career planning, learning strategies, and potential student development issues. More than one fourth of survey respondents (25.8%) administered an academic seminar with uniform academic content, followed closely by academic seminar on various topics (23.4%), basic study skills seminar (22.4%), and hybrid (22.4%). Lastly, preprofessional or discipline-linked seminar (14.4%) and other (2.5%) were the most underutilized seminar types reported by institutions within the aggregate.

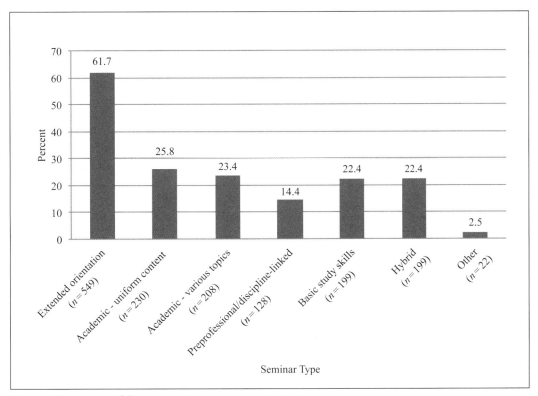

Figure 4. Percentage of discrete seminar type across institutions.

When institutional characteristics were taken into account, significant disparities began to emerge. Most notably, two-year institutions (74.9%) were significantly more likely to offer extended orientation seminars than four-year institutions (57.0%, $p < 0.01$). Similarly, public institutions offered extended orientation seminars far more frequently than private institutions (71.1% and 51.4%, respectively; $p < 0.01$). Significant differences ($p < 0.01$) also existed across first-year class size; as class size increased from less than 500 to more than 4,001, the use of extended orientation seminars also increased.

Though institutions most often reported extended orientation seminars as their campus' primary seminar type, this does not diminish the use of other seminar types. Four-year institutions were significantly more likely than community colleges ($p < 0.01$) to offer academic seminars on various topics (29.6% and 6.0%, respectively), preprofessional or discipline-linked seminars (16.2%

and 9.4%, respectively; $p < 0.01$), and hybrid seminars (24.0% and 17.9%, respectively; $p < 0.05$). However, community colleges offered basic study skills seminars more frequently than four-year institutions (39.2% and 16.3%, respectively; $p < 0.01$).

With regard to institutional control, public institutions were more than twice as likely as private institutions to offer preprofessional or discipline-linked seminars (18.8% and 9.6%, respectively; $p < 0.01$) and basic study skills seminars (30.0% and 14.1%, respectively; $p < 0.01$). However, private institutions offer academic seminars on various topics more frequently than public institutions (29.3% and 17.9% respectively; $p < 0.01$). Finally, as first-year class size increased from less than 500 to more than 4,001 across all institutions, the use of preprofessional or discipline-linked and basic study skills seminars increased significantly ($p < 0.01$).

Primary Seminar

As noted earlier, respondents were asked to identify the seminar type with the highest total first-year student enrollment. They were then asked to complete the remainder of the survey based on that seminar type, referred to as the primary seminar. Respondents overwhelmingly reported that the extended orientation seminar had the highest total student enrollment, followed by academic with uniform content, academic on various topics, hybrid, basic study skills, preprofessional or discipline-linked, and other (Figure 5). Many of these statistics remained nearly unchanged from the 2006 survey cycle. However, institutions reported offering twice as many preprofessional or discipline-linked seminars (1.6% in 2006 as compared to 3.7% in 2009) yet slightly fewer seminars categorized have been categorized as hybrid since 2006 (16.2% in 2006 compared to 15.3% in 2009). Caution should be taken when interpreting the decrease in hybrid seminars across college campuses given its introduction as an identifiable seminar type during the 2006 survey cycle.

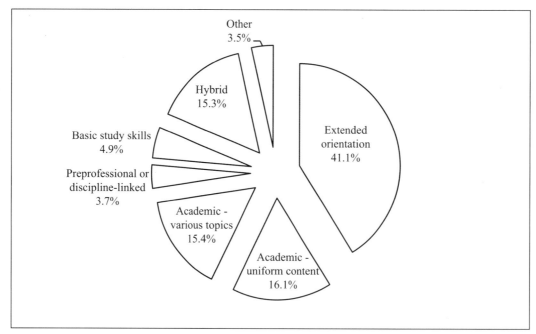

Figure 5. First-year seminar type with the highest total student enrollment ($n = 862$).

Disaggregating these data across institutional type and control uncovered a number of statistical differences (Figure 6). The most common primary seminar type within two-year institutions was extended orientation, followed by academic with uniform content and basic study skills. Comparatively, the primary seminar types within four-year institutions, in descending order, were extended orientation, academic on various topics, academic with uniform content, and hybrid. Community colleges were significantly ($p < 0.01$) more likely to administer basic study skills seminars compared to four-year institutions, while four-year institutions were significantly ($p < 0.01$) more likely to administer an academic seminar on various topics (19.9%) compared to community colleges.

Very similar results exist when disaggregating the data by institutional control. The primary seminar type within public institutions was extended orientation, followed by academic with uniform content and hybrid, whereas the primary seminars at private institutions were extended orientation, academic on various topics, and hybrid. Public institutions were significantly more likely to administer extended orientation seminars compared to private institutions, whereas private institutions were significantly more likely to administer an academic seminar on various topics compared to public institutions.

The distribution of primary seminar type across first-year class size is similar to the distribution for all seminar offerings. Larger institutions were significantly more likely to administer extended orientation seminars; whereas, smaller institutions were significantly more likely to administer

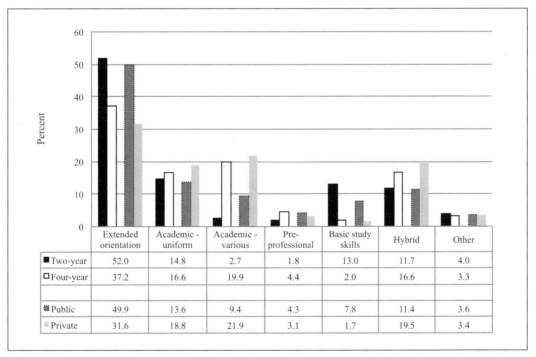

Figure 6. Seminar type with the highest total student enrollment across institutional type and control (all comparisons significant at $p < 0.01$, $n = 862$).

hybrid seminars. Though the distribution of primary seminar type across institutional size for academic with uniform content and academic on various topics were statistically significant, the distributions varied minimally and, thus, do not provide practical significance.

Required Versus Elective Seminars

Though 87.3% of the institutions surveyed reported having a first-year seminar, the extent to which first-year seminars are required varied across institutions. Table 2 outlines the two most extreme responses with regards to reporting the percentage of first-year students required to take a seminar: (a) institutions where the seminar was completely voluntary and (b) institutions were all students were required to participate. Survey responses showed that four-year institutions were significantly ($p < 0.01$) more likely to have the entire first-year class participate in a seminar compared to two-year institutions. Private institutions were nearly three times more likely to require all first-year students to participate in a seminar compared to public institutions; whereas, public institutions were three times more likely than private institutions to make the seminar voluntary for all students. The percentage of institutions that require the entire first-year class to participate in a seminar diminished as first-year class size increased. These data indicate that small, private institutions—that have high percentages of students enrolling in first-year seminars—were more likely to require the entire first-year class to participate in a first-year seminar, while large, public institutions were less likely to require students to take a first-year seminar.

Table 2
First-Year Students Required to Take the Primary First-Year Seminar

	Two-year	Four-year	Public	Private	Less than 500	501 - 1,000	1,001 - 2,000	2,001 - 3,000	3,001 - 4,000	4,001+
None	33.0	15.0	29.3	9.4	7.8	21.2	22.2	26.8	48.1	31.3
-	-	-	-	-	-	-	-	-	-	-
100%	19.5	46.7	20.9	59.7	55.4	46.8	28.7	22.5	19.2	9.4

Note. All comparisons significant at $p < 0.01$, ($n = 855$).

Student Groups Required to Take a Seminar

The versatile content and framework of first-year seminars provides institutions the opportunity to target specific student groups to address various needs. For example, first-generation students often enter college at a severe disadvantage with regard to navigating and recognizing the resources and services provided at a large, public four-year institution compared to their non-first-generation peers (Horn, Nunez, & Bobbitt, 2000; Terenzini, Springer, Yaeger, Pascarella, & Nora, 1996). As such, higher education professionals may be more likely to target these students and require them to enroll in an extended orientation seminar. Conversely, honors students are generally more likely to enter college academically prepared. Therefore, student affairs and academic professionals may permit honor students to forego enrolling in a seminar or require them to enroll in a specific type of seminar (e.g., academic or preprofessional). To measure the degree to which institutions target specific student groups, respondents were asked to identify which student groups were required to take a first-year seminar. Table 3 illustrates the significant differences in the percentage of each student group required to participate in a first-year seminar between two-year and four-year institutions. Two-year institutions were significantly ($p < 0.05$) more likely to require academically underprepared students and students within specific majors to participate in a seminar as compared to four-year institutions. These findings were, perhaps, not surprising as community colleges often serve students who need developmental education or enter a two-year program to obtain a very specific certificate or degree. Given the prominence of extended orientation, academic with uniform content, and basic study skills seminars, it is possible that students at two-year institutions are being required to take these types of seminars (see Figure 6, p. 13).

Table 3

Student Groups Required to Take the First-Year Seminar by Institutional Type

	Two-year	Four-year	Difference
Percentages larger for two-year			
None are required to take it[a]	30.2	13.7	16.5**
Academically underprepared students	18.3	13.0	5.3*
Other	14.9	9.8	5.1*
Students within specific majors	8.5	4.9	3.6*
TRIO participant	4.7	3.7	1.0
Percentages larger for four-year			
All first-year students are required to take it[a]	31.5	62.1	-30.6**
Provisionally admitted students	1.3	9.0	-7.7**
Honors students	2.1	7.8	-5.7**
Student-athletes	3.8	8.6	-4.8*
Learning community participants	3.8	8.4	-4.6*
Undeclared students	1.3	5.8	-4.5**
First-generation students	2.6	6.0	-3.4*
International students	1.7	4.7	-3.0*
Transfer students	3.0	6.0	-3.0
Preprofessional students	0.9	3.8	-2.7*
Students residing within a particular residence hall	0.4	2.9	-2.5*
Students participating in dual-enrollment programs	1.3	1.8	-0.5

[a] The percentages of students required and not required differ from the percentages in Table 2. These differences exist because data are from two separate questions.
*$p < 0.05$. **$p < 0.01$.

Similarly, four-year institutions targeted unique student groups to take a first-year seminar. Compared to two-year institutions, provisionally admitted students, honors students, student-athletes, learning community participants, undeclared students, first-generation students, international students, preprofessional students, and students residing within a particular residence hall were significantly more likely to be required to take a seminar at four-year institutions. Many of these student groups are typically more prevalent at four-year institutions (e.g., learning community participants, students residing within a particular residence hall), which may help explain the significant differences between two- and four-year institutions. Among the 2009 National Survey participants, it appears that four-year institutions require first-year seminars for a greater number of student groups.[4]

Table 4 illustrates the significant differences among the percentages of student groups required to participate in a first-year seminar between public and private institutions. Similar to two-year institutions, public institutions were more likely to require academically underprepared students to enroll in a seminar compared to private institutions. In addition to academically underprepared students, public institutions were significantly more likely than private institutions to require students within specific majors and TRIO participants to enroll in a seminar.

Survey responses indicated that private institutions were more likely than public institutions to require transfer students and first-generation students to enroll in a seminar. These two student groups are theoretically more likely to be sensitive to new institutional environments and practices. Therefore, these results suggest that private institutions may recognize the potential disadvantages these students have entering college and make an additional effort to acclimate the students to campus and academic life. One possible mechanism to do this would be through the use of an extended orientation seminar, though private institutions are less likely to offer these seminar types. This suggests there may be a disconnect between serving specific student populations and the type of seminar or objectives of the seminar, which is addressed in more detail in the Assessing the Seminar section.

Interestingly, international students were not heavily targeted as a student group required to participate in a seminar by campuses in the 2009 sample regardless of institutional type or control. This is somewhat surprising given that international students are more likely not to be native English speakers and may find it difficult to navigate and adjust to a uniquely different national culture and environment, let alone an American college campus (Kaczmarek, Matlock, Merta, Ames, & Ross, 1994). When international students were required to take the seminar, those at private institutions were slightly more likely to be required to do so than those at public institutions. Future research is needed to investigate the benefits (or disadvantages) first-year seminars may provide international students.

---

[4] Caution should be taken when interpreting these significant results because of the low sample sizes (and subsequent low percentages) within student group comparisons (e.g., preprofessional students at two-year institutions ($n = 2$, 0.9%) and four-year institutions ($n = 25$, 3.8%), respectively).

Table 4
Student Groups Required to Take the First-Year Seminar by Institutional Control

	Public	Private	Difference
Percentages larger for public			
None are required to take it[a]	26.3	9.2	17.1**
Academically underprepared students	19.0	9.4	9.6**
Students within specific majors	8.2	3.3	4.9**
TRIO participants	6.3	1.4	4.9**
Other	13.2	8.9	4.3*
Learning community participants	8.2	6.1	2.1
Provisionally admitted students	7.5	6.3	1.2
Student-athletes	7.8	6.8	1
Students residing within a particular residence hall	2.6	1.9	0.7
Percentages larger for private			
All first-year students are required to take it[a]	31.5	78.6	-47.1**
Transfer students	2.6	8.0	-5.4**
First-generation students	3.0	7.3	-4.3**
International students	2.4	5.6	-3.2**
Preprofessional students	1.7	4.5	-2.8*
Undeclared students	3.7	5.6	-1.9
Honors students	6.0	6.6	-0.6
Students participating in dual-enrollment programs	1.5	1.9	0.4

[a] The percentages of students required and not required differ from the percentages in Table 2 because these data are from two separate questions.
*$p < 0.05$. **$p < 0.01$.

Special Sections Offered for Subpopulations

Survey respondents were asked to identify *unique subpopulations of students for whom special sections of the first-year seminar are offered.* Approximately 43% of respondents reported that no special sections were offered. Of the remaining, 57% who reported that at least one special section of a first-year seminar served a unique subpopulation of students, the responses varied by institutional type and control.

Community colleges were significantly more likely to offer a special section to first-year students participating in dual enrollment programs compared to four-year institutions (Table 5), though the difference was marginal (3.5 percentage points, $p < 0.01$). Conversely, four-year institutions were significantly more likely to offer a special section to honor students, with a substantial difference of 19.3 percentage points ($p < 0.01$). Though the percent differences were marginal, a number of special sections serving unique subpopulations of first-year students were significantly greater at four-year institutions compared to community colleges, including undeclared students, students within specific majors, transfer students, provisionally admitted students, preprofessional students, and students residing within a particular residence hall.

Table 5

Special Sections of the First-Year Seminar for Subpopulations by Institutional Type

	Two-year	Four-year	Difference
Percentages larger for two-year			
Academically underprepared students	21.3	15.9	5.4
Students participating in dual-enrollment programs	4.3	0.8	3.5**
Learning community participants	19.6	16.6	2.9
Other (please specify)	11.1	8.4	2.7
No special sections are offered	44.3	42.3	2.0
First-generation students	4.3	2.4	1.9
TRIO participants	5.5	4.3	1.2
Percentages larger for four-year			
Honors students	5.1	24.4	-19.3**
Undeclared students	2.1	7.8	-5.7**
Students within specific majors	8.9	14.5	-5.6*
Transfer students	1.7	7.2	-5.5**
Provisionally admitted students	0.4	5.2	-4.8**
Preprofessional students (e.g., prelaw, premed)	1.7	6.3	-4.6**
Students residing within a particular residence hall	0.0	4.3	-4.3**
Student-athletes	5.5	8.2	-2.7
International students	3.8	4.0	0.2

*$p < 0.05$. **$p < 0.01$.

Over half of private institutions reported that no special sections were offered to unique subpopulations of students, a significant difference ($p < 0.01$) compared to their public institution peers. The special sections within a seminar that were significantly more likely to be found at a public institution compared to a private institution were extensive (Table 6). However, it is important to note that public institutions had a significantly larger percentage of special sections for a wide range of student populations. These student populations included high achieving, disciplinary interests, and declared preprofessionals. In other words, public institutions are utilizing the seminar to specifically target a full spectrum of undergraduates.

Table 6
Special Sections of the First-Year Seminar for Subpopulations by Institutional Control

	Public	Private	Difference
Percentages larger for public			
Learning community participants	25.9	8.2	17.6**
Student-athletes	12.5	2.1	10.4**
Students within specific majors	17.9	7.8	10.1**
Academically underprepared students	20.7	13.6	7.1**
TRIO participants	8.0	0.9	7.0**
Undeclared students	9.3	3.1	6.2**
Other (please specify)	11.6	6.3	5.3**
Preprofessional students (e.g., prelaw, premed)	7.1	2.8	4.3**
Students residing within a particular residence hall	4.5	1.6	2.9**
Students participating in dual-enrollment programs	3.0	0.2	2.8**
Provisionally admitted students	5.2	2.6	2.6*
First-generation students	4.1	1.6	2.5*
International students	5.0	2.8	2.1
Percentages larger for private			
No special sections are offered	34.5	51.9	-17.4**
Honors students	17.9	20.9	-3.0
Transfer students	5.6	5.9	-0.3

*$p < 0.05$. **$p < 0.01$.

Seminar Class Size

It is important to note that the terms *first-year class size* (i.e., the number of entering first-year students at the institution) and *seminar class size* (i.e., the number of students enrolled in the first-year seminar) are not interchangeable. This section focuses solely on the number of students who enrolled in the first-year seminar. Respondents were asked to identify the approximate class size for each section of the primary seminar. While the Survey included a full range of six response options for class size, the analyses dichotomize this variable into *19 or less* and *20 or greater* to reflect the thresholds of class size generally used in practice and college rankings. In the aggregate, the percentage of first-year seminar class size was normally distributed. A number of patterns emerged when the data were disaggregated across institutional type, control, and size. As shown in Figure 7, two-year institutions were significantly more likely ($p < 0.01$) to have seminar class sizes larger than 20 students compared to four-year institutions. Furthermore, four-year institutions were equally likely to have seminar classes with fewer than 19 students and with more than 20 students. Public institutions were more likely ($p < 0.01$) to have seminar class sizes larger than 20 students compared to private institutions. The distribution of seminar class size at community colleges is nearly identical to the distribution of public institutions. Examination of the distribution of seminar class size across institutional type and control shows that private institutions were more likely to administer seminars with lower class sizes.

Figure 8 displays the percentage of seminar class size by first-year class size. As first-year class size increased, seminar class sizes were more likely to increase. Institutions with a first-year enrollment of 501-1,000 students were nearly as likely to have seminar classes with fewer than 19 students

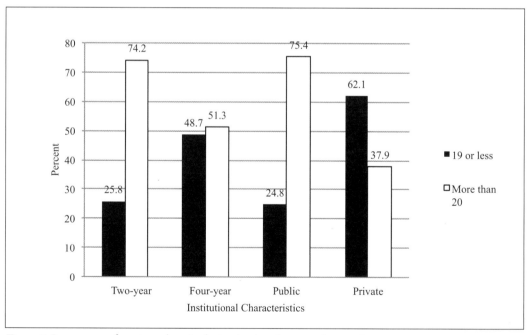

Figure 7. Percentage of seminar class size by institutional type and control.

(46.3%) as they were to have seminars with more than 20 students (53.7%). However, when first-year enrollment reaches 1,001-2,000 students, institutions were twice as likely ($p < 0.01$) to have class sizes of more than 20 students as class sizes under 19 (66.7% and 33.3%, respectively). The difference becomes even more prominent as first-year enrollment reaches 2,001-3,000 and 3,001-4,000 students. Institutions with first-year enrollments at these levels were four times more likely ($p < 0.01$) to have seminar classes with more than 20 students compared to fewer than 19 students.

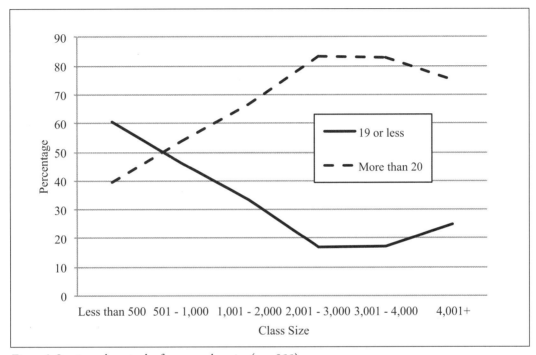

Figure 8. Seminar class size by first-year class size ($n = 855$).

Course Objectives

The type of first-year seminar an institution implements can be a telling piece of information, often revealing how an institution views the purpose of the seminar. However, the type of seminar an institution implements differs from the course objectives set forth by the institution for its seminar. While some overlap is likely to exist, course objectives more clearly reflect the strategic academic and social skills institutions expect their first-year students to acquire. Examining the data in the aggregate, respondents identified the following as the three most important course objectives:[5] (a) developing academic skills, (b) developing a connection with the institution, and (c) providing an orientation to various campus resources and services.

---

[5] Respondents were only able to select up to three course objectives.

Table 7 illustrates the most important course objectives for the first-year seminar by institutional type. It is worth noting that both two-year and four-year institutions place great importance on developing academic skills and developing a connection with the institution as course objectives. More than two thirds (66.4%) of the respondents from two-year institutions reported that the most important course objective is to provide orientation to various campus resources and services compared to only 40.9% of their four-year counterparts that identified this objective as most important. Two-year institutions also selected self-exploration or personal development and developing financial literacy as important course objectives at significantly ($p < 0.01$) higher rates than four-year institutions.

Table 7
Most Important Course Objectives by Institutional Type

	Two-year	Four-year	Difference
Percentages larger for two-year			
Provide orientation to campus resources and services	66.4	40.9	25.5**
Self-exploration/personal development	37.0	25.5	11.5**
Develop academic skills	57.0	53.7	3.3
Develop financial literacy	3.0	0.5	2.5**
Develop a connection with the institution	51.5	49.8	1.7
Percentages larger for four-year			
Increase student/faculty interaction	6.0	20.8	-14.8**
Create common first-year experience	14.9	26.3	-11.4**
Develop writing skills	6.4	13.9	-7.5**
Introduce a discipline	2.1	8.7	-6.6**
Improve sophomore return rates	11.9	16.8	-4.9
Other	5.5	9.0	-3.5
Develop support network/friendships	14.9	18.3	-3.4
Encourage arts participation	0.4	0.6	-0.2

**$p < 0.01$.

Four-year institutions place significantly ($p < 0.01$) more emphasis on increasing student/faculty interaction as an important course objective compared to two-year institutions. Furthermore, more than one fourth of four-year institutions (26.3%) reported that creating a common first-year experience is an important course objective, a significant ($p < 0.01$) difference compared to two-year institutions (14.9%). Combined, these two findings suggest that four-year institutions use the first-year seminar as a mechanism to integrate students into the college milieu. By introducing theoretically vetted good practices (Pascarella et al., 2006; Pascarella, Wolniak, Cruce, & Blaich,

2004), such as student/faculty interaction, four-year institutions may increase the likelihood of student persistence (Tinto, 1993; Upcraft, Gardner, & Associates, 1989; Upcraft, Gardner, Barefoot, & Associates, 2005). Finally, four-year institutions identified developing writing skills and introducing a discipline as important course objectives when compared with community colleges, though the differences were statistically but not practically significant.

Similar trends in course objectives existed between public and private institutions, as illustrated in Table 8. For example, public institutions placed a greater importance on providing orientation to campus resources and services as a course objective compared to private institutions, yielding a significant difference of 17.1%. Public institutions placed a greater importance on developing academic skills as a course objective compared to private institutions. Private institutions were significantly ($p < 0.01$) more likely to identify the development of writing skills, creating a common first-year experience, and increasing student/faculty interaction as important course objectives compared to public institutions. It is important to note that both public and private institutions selected developing a connection with the institution as a vital course objective.

Table 8
Most Important Course Objectives by Institutional Control

	Public	Private	Difference
Percentages larger for public			
Provide orientation to campus resources and services	55.8	38.7	17.1**
Develop academic skills	58.2	50.7	7.5*
Develop a connection with the institution	51.9	48.4	3.5
Improve sophomore return rates	16.6	14.3	2.3
Develop financial literacy	1.9	0.2	1.7*
Self-exploration/personal development	29.1	27.9	1.2
Percentages larger for private			
Develop writing skills	5.8	18.5	-12.7**
Create common first-year experience	17.5	29.6	-12.1**
Increase student/faculty interaction	12.9	21.1	-8.2**
Other	6.7	9.6	-2.9
Develop support network/friendships	16.4	18.5	-2.1
Introduce a discipline	6.7	7.3	-0.6
Encourage arts participation	0.4	0.7	-0.3

*$p < 0.05$. **$p < 0.01$.

Table 9 reinforces the importance colleges and universities place on developing a connection with the institution, developing academic skills, and providing an orientation to campus resources and services as important course objectives, even across unique seminar types. Developing academic skills was viewed as one of the three most important course objective across all six seminar types, with developing a connection with the institution and orientation to campus resources and services recognized as the other two most important objectives across five of the six seminar types. Institutions that implement academic seminars on various topics as their primary seminar deviated from their colleagues, identifying the increase in student/faculty interaction as an important course objective. Similarly, half of the institutions that implement preprofessional or discipline-linked seminars identified introduction to a discipline as one of their primary course objectives. Nonetheless, the overwhelming evidence suggests that all institutions place significant value on three important course objectives: (a) developing a connection with the institution, (b) developing academic skills, and (c) providing an orientation to various campus resources and services.

Table 9
Three Most Important Course Objectives Across Seminar Type

	Extended orientation	Academic– uniform content	Academic– various topics	Pre- professional	Basic study skills	Hybrid
Develop connection with institution	59.9%	45.3%	39.9%		47.6%	51.5%
Develop academic skills	45.5%	67.6%	66.2%	40.6%	88.1%	58.3%
Increase student/ faculty interaction			39.9%			
Orientation to campus resources and services	65.3%	38.1%[a]		50.0%	54.8%	51.5%
Introduce a discipline				50.0%		

[a] 38.1% of institutions offering academic seminars with uniform content also indicated self-exploration/ personal development as an important course objective. $p < 0.01$.

Seminar Topics

There is a distinct difference between the course objective of a first-year seminar and the topics taught within the seminar. Seminar topics and curriculum content tend to reveal how colleges and universities define their seminar, often representing the vehicles through which seminars achieve their course goals. Within the aggregate, the three most highly reported seminar topics by institutions were (a) *campus resources* (42.4%), (b) *study skills* (39.8%), and (c) *academic planning/advising* (35.7%). As a reminder, when the data were analyzed in the aggregate, the three most important course objectives were *develop academic skills* (54.6%), *develop connection with the institution* (50.2%), and *provide orientation to various campus resources and services* (47.6%).

Whereas institutions clearly identify the development of academic skills as a primary course objective, institutions specified campus resources, study skills, and academic planning as content-driven support for the course objective.

Table 10 illustrates the most frequently reported topics in the seminar by institutional type. Survey respondents indicated that two-year institutions were significantly ($p < 0.01$) and substantially more likely to incorporate study skills content within the seminar compared to four-year institutions. Over half (56.2%) of the community colleges reported including campus resources within the seminar content compared to only 37.4% of their four-year counterparts. Community colleges were also statistically more likely ($p < 0.01$) to integrate academic planning or advising and time management content within the seminar compared to four-year institutions.

Conversely, four-year institutions were far more likely to introduce critical thinking as a topic for a seminar compared to community colleges. Four-year institutions were 10 times more likely to incorporate a specific disciplinary topic into the seminar compared to community colleges. This suggests that four-year institutions place a substantially greater emphasis on disciplinary issues (e.g., academic dishonesty) within the first-year seminar compared to community colleges. Four-year institutions also reported integrating writing skills as a component of the seminar at a far greater rate than community colleges and were more likely to include diversity issues in the curriculum compared to community colleges.

Table 10
Most Commonly Reported Seminar Topics by Institutional Type

	Two-year	**Four-year**	**Difference**
Percentages larger for two-year			
Study skills	59.6	32.7	26.9**
Campus resources	56.2	37.4	18.8**
Academic planning/advising	43.4	33.0	10.4**
Time management	34.5	25.2	9.3**
Career exploration/preparation	18.3	14.5	3.8
College policies and procedures	17.9	14.1	3.8
Financial literacy	1.3	0.9	0.4
Percentages larger for four-year			
Critical thinking	18.7	40.6	-21.9**
Specific disciplinary topic	1.7	18.5	-16.8**
Writing skills	5.5	21.5	-16.0**
Other	7.7	17.4	-9.7**
Diversity issues	1.3	8.9	-7.6**
Relationship issues	7.2	9.9	-2.7
Health and wellness	2.6	4.1	-1.6

**$p < 0.01$.

Table 11 illustrates the most commonly reported topics comprising seminar content by institutional control. Of particular interest is the similarity between two-year and public institutions and between four-year and private institutions with respect to course content. With the exception of college policies and procedures, two-year and public institutions and four-year and private institutions reported including specific seminar topics at nearly identical rates.

More specifically, public institutions were far more likely to integrate campus resources as a topic within the seminar compared to private institutions. Nearly half of the public institutions also identified study skills as an important course topic, which is significantly ($p < 0.01$) higher than their private counterparts. Public institutions were significantly ($p < 0.01$) more likely than private institutions to incorporate academic planning or advising, time management, and career exploration or preparation into their seminar content.

Private institutions, however, were three times more likely ($p < 0.01$) to integrate writing skills within the seminar compared to public institutions. Critical thinking was also of greater importance as a seminar topic for private institutions compared to public institutions. Private institutions were also significantly ($p < 0.01$) more likely than public institutions to include specific disciplinary topics and relationship issues into the seminar content.

Table 11

Most Commonly Reported Seminar Topics by Institutional Control

	Public	**Private**	**Difference**
Percentages larger for public			
Campus resources	51.7	32.2	19.6**
Study skills	48.3	30.5	17.8**
Academic planning/advising	39.9	31.2	8.7**
Time management	31.5	23.5	8.0**
Career exploration/preparation	18.1	12.7	5.4*
Financial literacy	1.5	0.5	1.0
Percentages larger for private			
Writing skills	8.4	27.0	-18.6**
Critical thinking	27.2	43.2	-16.0**
Specific disciplinary topic	9.9	18.5	-8.6**
Relationship issues	5.4	13.4	-8.0**
Other	11.0	19.0	-8.0**
Diversity issues	5.8	8.0	-2.2
College policies and procedures	14.2	16.0	-1.7
Health and wellness	3.0	4.5	-1.4

*$p < 0.05$. **$p < 0.01$.

When the most reported topics included in first-year seminar content were examined across first-year class size, few significant differences exist. Moreover, the cases within each cell were often below the accepted 10 case minimum. As such, comparisons across first-year class size yielded only one topic of practical significance. As first-year class size decreased, institutions were more likely to report that an introduction to campus resources was an important topic within their seminar. In other words, smaller first-year class sizes were more likely to incorporate campus resources within the seminar content.

Table 12 illustrates the distribution of the three most reported topics that comprise the first-year seminar content across each seminar type. The most reported topics across all seminar types—defined by counting the number of occupied cells horizontally—were study skills, academic planning, campus resources, and critical thinking. The most reported topics across the six unique seminar types tend to align with the definition and purpose of the seminar type. For example, it should be expected that the three most important topics incorporated into an extended orientation seminar would be academic planning or advising, campus resources, and study skills. All three of these topics are often explored and taught within an extended orientation seminar. Another example is the incorporation of critical thinking, specific disciplinary topic, and writing skills within academic seminar on various topics.

Table 12

Most Commonly Reported Seminar Topics by Seminar Type

	Extended orientation	Academic–uniform content	Academic–various topics	Pre-professional	Basic study skills	Hybrid
Academic planning/advising	46.1%			50.0%	47.6%	
Career exploration/preparation				50.0%		
Campus resources	61.3%	31.7%				43.9%
Critical thinking		51.8%	77.4%			37.1%
Specific disciplinary topic			52.6%	46.9%		
Study skills	46.3%	40.3%			83.3%	45.5%
Writing skills			52.6%			
Time management					47.6%	

p < 0.01.

Structural Characteristics of Administering the Seminar

The administration of the first-year seminar is as diverse as first-year seminar characteristics across institutional type, control, size, and seminar type. First-year seminars are expected to juggle many institutional goals, including orientation, community building, introducing campus resources, and the like. To better understand how seminars are structured to undertake and organize these tasks, the 2009 Survey asked which administrative unit houses the first-year seminar and who oversees the seminars' objectives and performance standards. This section chronicles the seminars' length and classroom contact hours and examines how seminars are graded and credits are awarded as an academic unit within the college curriculum.

Administrative Unit

It is important to note that the response set for the survey question measuring the campus unit that directly administered the seminar in the 2009 Survey varied from previous administrations. The response *college or school* was added to the 2009 Survey, which may account for the shift in responses from 2006 to 2009, reported below. Results from the 2006 Survey found that 50.8% of respondents identified the division of academic affairs as the administrative unit for the first-year seminar, and only 10.5% identified a first-year program office as the administrative unit. Results from the 2009 Survey suggest that while the first-year program office remained consistently low (11.9%) as the administrative unit, 37% of survey respondents reported that academic affairs was the administrative unit for the seminar, a drop of 13.8% over three years. A potential explanation for this precipitous drop was the addition of *college or school* as a response option within the 2009 Survey. Respondents may have been able to more accurately categorize the administrative unit of their seminar than in years past. The remaining administrative units were relatively consistent from 2006 to 2009 (Figure 9).

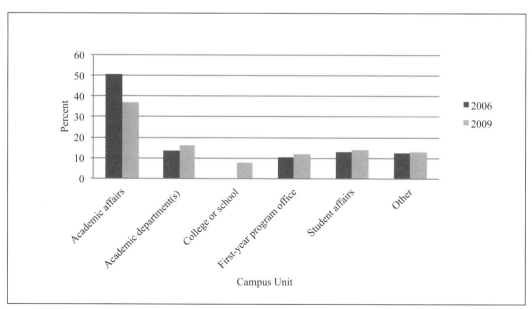

Figure 9. Campus unit responsible for administering the seminar (*n* = 847).

Two-year institutions were three times more likely ($p < 0.01$) to administer the seminar through an academic department (32.9%) compared to four-year institutions (10.5%). Examples of academic departments that administered the seminar at community colleges included developmental studies, counseling, general education, and student success. Four-year institutions were four times more likely ($p < 0.01$) to administer the seminar through a first-year program office (14.8%) compared to two-year institutions (3.7%). The majority of four-year institutions administered the seminar through the division of academic affairs (39.3%), significantly more ($p < 0.01$) than their community college peers (30.1%). The majority of survey respondents from both public and private institutions indicated that the division of academic affairs administered the seminar (31.0% and 43.5%, respectively). Yet, the number of institutions that administered the seminar through the division of academic affairs decreased as first-year class size increased from less than 500 (45.1%) to more than 4,001 (21.9%). Public institutions (20.8%) were significantly more likely ($p < 0.01$) to administer the seminar through an academic department(s) compared to private institutions (11.5%), as were institutions with larger first-year classes (26.6% at 4,001+) compared to smaller first-year classes (13.7% at less than 500). Interestingly, when the variable measuring administrative unit was analyzed by seminar type, no distinctive patterns emerged. The division of academic affairs remained the predominate administrative unit regardless of seminar type.

Approximately three quarters (75.1%) of the survey respondents reported that the seminar has a dean, director, or coordinator. Four-year institutions (79.0%) and private institutions (80.0%) were significantly more likely ($p < 0.01$) than two-year institutions (63.9%) and public institutions (70.5%), respectively, to have a dean, director, or coordinator leading the seminar. Approximately two thirds (62.3%) of respondents reported that the dean, director, or coordinator was a part-time position, with 97.7% of part-time administrators holding another position on campus. These other roles included academic affairs administrator (28.6%), faculty member (30.1%), student affairs administrator (28.1%), and/or other (27.5%).

Length of Seminar

More than two thirds (67.8%) of all participating institutions reported the first-year seminar was one semester in length. At the remaining institutions, length varied from half a semester (12.6%), one quarter (5.9%), and one year (3.8%). Approximately 10% of institutions reported an *other* seminar length, with write-in responses varying in scope from three-day weekend models to multiweek sections. Two-year institutions were significantly more likely ($p < 0.01$) to offer a half a semester (18.3%) or one quarter (7.8%) class compared to four-year institutions (10.7% and 5.2%, respectively). Comparatively, four-year institutions (4.9%) were nearly 10 times more likely ($p < 0.01$) than community colleges (0.5%) to administer a one-year section of the first-year seminar. Interestingly, no significant differences existed across seminar type.

The total classroom contact hours per week distributed fairly evenly across institutional type, control, size, and seminar type, though a handful of patterns emerged. The majority of survey respondents indicated that three classroom contact hours were held per week (38.8%), followed by one contact hour (26.7%), two contact hours (25.4%), four contact hours (6.0%), and more than five (3.2%). Four-year institutions (7.8%) were significantly more likely ($p < 0.01$) than community colleges (0.9%) to maintain four contact hours per week, as were private institutions (11.5%) compared to public institutions (0.9%). Academic seminars on various topics (67.9%) and basic study skill seminars (61.0%) were significantly more likely ($p < 0.01$) to maintain three classroom contact hours per week compared to the other types.

Seminar Grades and Credit

Approximately four fifths (80.5%) of survey respondents indicated that the first-year seminar was letter graded, which is comparable to respondents on the 2006 Survey (82.0%). Thirteen percent of survey respondents reported their seminar was pass/fail, with 2.5% reporting the seminar was not graded and 4.0% provided *other* grading. Public institutions (84.9%) were significantly more likely ($p < 0.01$) than private institutions (75.6%) to provide letter grades, whereas private institutions (17.3%) were significantly more likely ($p < 0.01$) to grade the seminar as pass/fail compared to public institutions (8.9%). Across seminar types, both academic with uniform content (89.9%) and academic on various topics (89.3%) seminars were significantly more likely ($p < 0.01$) to provide letter grading for the course compared to other seminar types.

In the aggregate, 91.3% of survey respondents reported that the first-year seminar carries academic credit. This suggests an overwhelming majority of higher education institutions view the first-year seminar as a valuable curriculum resource that merits academic credit. Of the reporting institutions, 43.3% awarded one credit for the class, 14.1% awarded two credits, 31.9% awarded three credits, and 10.7% awarded four credits or more. In particular, academic seminars on various topics were three times more likely ($p < 0.01$) to award four credits compared to all other seminar types.

More than half (53.1%) of the participating institutions indicated that the seminar credit is applied toward general education requirements, 39.8% toward an elective, 9.7% toward a major requirement, and 9.4% toward *other*. Four-year institutions (59.8%) and private institutions (71.9%) were significantly more likely ($p < 0.01$ and $p < 0.05$, respectively) to apply seminar credit toward general education requirements compared to community colleges (33%) and public institutions (35.9%), respectively. Conversely, community colleges (59.8%) and public institutions (58.9%) were significantly more likely ($p < 0.01$) to apply seminar credit as an elective compared to four-year institutions (33.1%) and private institutions (18.9%), respectively. Institutions with larger first-year class sizes were significantly ($p < 0.01$) more likely to apply the seminar credit as an elective; whereas, institutions with smaller first-year class sizes applied (though nonsignificant) seminar credit toward general education (Figure 10). Across seminar types, both academic with uniform content (64.7%) and academic on various topics (75.2%) seminars were significantly more likely ($p < 0.01$) to apply course credit toward general education requirements compared to other types. Exactly half (50.0%) of preprofessional or discipline-linked seminars applied credit toward major requirements, more than five times the total sample's average.

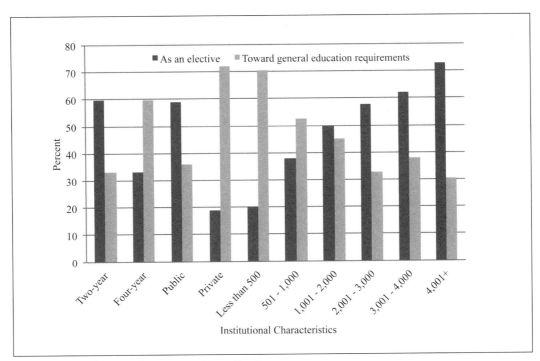

Figure 10. Distribution of seminar credit application.

Conclusion

As this section illustrates, institutions continue to define their first-year seminar in a variety of unique ways while enrolling a large proportion of their first-year population into a seminar. When students take a first-year seminar, it is likely to be an extended orientation seminar, as this continues to be the dominant type reported. Seminar class sizes were likely to be larger than 20 students, except at private institutions where seminars were significantly smaller. While institutions vary greatly on identifying student populations required to participate in a seminar and topics within the seminar, overwhelming evidence exists that all institutions place significant value on developing a connection with the institution, developing academic skills, and providing an orientation to campus resources and services as important course objectives within the seminar.

An emerging theme throughout this section is that no one administrative unit is responsible for the first-year seminar at all institutions. Though the division of academic affairs is the primary administrative unit at many institutions, roughly half of the surveyed institutions identified another administrative unit under which the seminar is housed. Institutions also varied in reported seminar course length and total classroom contact hours. One consistent measure across institutions was the application of letter grading and awarding of academic credit. These findings suggest that while institutions vary on the administration of first-year seminars, institutions overwhelming support the seminar as a valid academic program by awarding a letter grade and academic credit for students' participation.

Instruction and Pedagogy

The previous sections of this research brief have highlighted the history of first-year seminars in American higher education, offered a typology for understanding the different elements of these courses, and provided current information about their administration and characteristics. However, the first-year seminar is comprised of so much more than type and structural characteristics. The total impact of a course is entirely reliant upon what happens inside the framework of these organizational elements, most notably at the hand of the instructor and via the pedagogical elements that she or he employs in the course.

Although the range of instructional and pedagogical decisions in a course is wide, the 2009 National Survey of First-Year Seminars continued to collect data about some of the most fundamental aspects of instruction, including who teaches the first-year seminar, how the position as seminar instructor fits into the workload of higher education professionals, as well as how instructors are trained and compensated for their efforts in the first-year seminar classroom. Further, the Survey captured both quantitative and open-ended data on instructional practices and structures that are commonly paired with a first-year seminar, such as online learning, service-learning, and linked courses. The data provide national context and illustrate common practices with respect to teaching and pedagogy in first-year seminar classrooms, thereby providing information to help guide campus-based decision making regarding these important aspects of first-year seminar development and administration.

Professional Role of First-Year Seminar Instructors

The 2009 National Survey included the question, *Who teaches the first-year seminar*, and allowed respondents to mark as many of the seven specific categories of campus professionals serving as instructors as was appropriate for their first-year seminar (Table 13). While most campus respondents marked multiple categories for this survey item, data analyses show that first-year seminar teaching responsibilities most often reside in the hands of full-time faculty. More than 60% of responding institutions reported that tenure-track faculty taught the first-year seminar, and well over 50% indicated that full-time, non-tenure-track faculty members were employed as seminar instructors. Student affairs professionals and adjunct faculty were also primary sources of the teaching pool for these first-year seminars. Comparatively, graduate and undergraduate students are still underrepresented among seminar instructors.

Table 13
First-Year Seminar Teaching Responsibility (n = 853)

Instructor for seminar	Percent
Tenure-track faculty	61.4
Full-time, non-tenure-track faculty	54.4
Student affairs professionals	48.2
Adjunct faculty	46.0
Other campus professionals	29.9
Graduate students	5.6
Undergraduate students	5.1

Note. Percentages can equal more than 100% because respondents were allowed to mark more than one category.

When these national data were disaggregated, analyses revealed that two-year campuses used adjunct faculty as instructors in first-year seminars at a significantly ($p < 0.01$) higher rate (61.7%) than four-year campuses (40.3%) and two-year campuses comparatively underutilized instructors from every other category with the most significant disparity emerging for tenure-track faculty (41.7% compared to 68.4%). Similarly, public institutions employed adjunct faculty as first-year seminar instructors more often than private institutions (55.0% vs. 36.2%) and used tenure-track faculty much less frequently than private institutions (57.3% vs. 65.7%). However, public colleges and universities in this sample more often engaged student affairs professionals (52.6%) and graduate students (8.0%) in first-year seminar classrooms than private institutions (43.4% and 3.1%, respectively).

For the most part, the size of an institution's first-year class did not have a significant relationship with who served as an instructor in the seminar. Chi-squared and bivariate correlation analyses found statistically significant relationships between only three of the seven types of instructors and size of the first-year student body: (a) adjunct faculty ($r = 0.16$, $p < 0.01$); (b) graduate student instructors ($r = 0.16$, $p < .01$); and (c) student affairs professionals ($r = 0.10$, $p < 0.01$). In all three instances, there was a slight positive relationship, meaning that institutions with larger first-year classes were more likely to use these types of instructors in first-year seminars than institutions with a smaller first-year class.

Analyses of instructors by seminar type yielded statistically significant differences across every category (Table 14). However, these results reflected a consistent overall pattern in which full-time faculty (both tenure-track and nontenure track) tended to serve as instructors more frequently for preprofessional seminars, academic seminars with uniform content, hybrid courses, and especially for academic seminars on various topics. Given the academic or discipline-specific nature of the objectives and content of these types of first-year seminars, this finding is perhaps not surprising. Conversely, student affairs professionals have a slightly higher representation in extended orientation seminars. Again, given that these professionals represent various campus units and have knowledge of a range of campus resources, the differences denote a good match between the skill set of the higher educators serving as instructors and the purposes of these specific types of seminars.

Table 14
First-Year Seminar Instructor Professional Responsibility by Seminar Type (n = 853)

	Extended orientation	Academic–uniform content	Academic–various topics	Pre-professional	Basic study skills	Hybrid
Tenure-track faculty**	54.5	68.4	90.2	68.8	35.7	67.4
Full-time, non-tenure-track faculty*	53.4	62.6	63.9	62.5	35.7	55.3
Student affairs professionals**	61.0	46.8	25.6	46.9	33.3	53.0
Adjunct faculty**	51.7	49.6	41.4	28.1	64.3	42.4
Other campus professionals**	35.9	26.6	20.3	34.4	19.1	33.3
Graduate students	7.9	2.9	3.0	9.4	4.8	6.8
Undergraduate students*	3.5	2.2	1.5	12.5	2.4	7.6

*$p < 0.05$. **$p < 0.01$.

Additional analyses show that organizing the findings into discrete categories of instructor type does not always show the full picture. In fact, 43.6% of institutions reported that at least some sections of first-year seminars were taught with an instructional team, and 8.6% of the respondents indicated that that all sections were taught via a team-teaching model. Analyses of nearly 350 open-ended survey responses revealed that these teaching teams tended to include one or two primary instructors with several other professionals serving as instructional support in areas of expertise (e.g., guest lecturers) or mentorship pairings, such as advisor to advisee, mentor within major, student peer mentor, or even mentoring of a new instructor by an experienced instructor. In a few instances, campuses had integrated a coaching team model that was inclusive of faculty, advisors, peers, and content experts for a first-year seminar section.

There was very little evidence of statistically significant differences in use of team teaching as a strategy across institutional characteristics (i.e., type, control, or size). Further, in the rare occasions that undergraduates were engaged as teachers for first-year seminars (5.1%), it was most often as a part of a team-teaching model.

The 2009 Survey also asked about the participation of academic advisors as instructors for their advisees' sections of first-year seminars. Approximately, one third of institutions (31.2%) report that at least some students are intentionally placed in sections taught by their academic advisor, although the proportion of students who are placed in sections taught by their advisor at responding institutions varies significantly (Figure 11). The practice of placing first-year students in seminars taught by their academic advisor was more common at four-year institutions than at two-year campuses (35.2% vs. 19.6%) as well as at private colleges and universities as compared to public institutions (35.4% and 27.3%, respectively). While practically meaningful, these differences did not reach statistical significance. Similar analyses also did not yield statistically significant differences in this practice across first-year class size or seminar type.

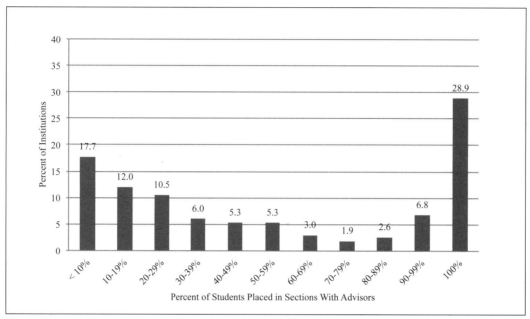

Figure 11. Percentage of students placed in sections with their advisors (*n* = 266).

Teaching Workload and Compensation

The Survey also inquired about how the responsibilities of teaching a first-year seminar fit into the overall professional workload and remuneration for instructors. As shown in Figure 12, tenure-track faculty at responding institutions taught first-year seminars as a part of their regular teaching load more frequently than as an overload. Similarly, the few graduate students who taught the course more often did so as an assigned responsibility. Conversely, instruction in a first-year seminar fell outside the parameters of assigned responsibilities for most student affairs professionals at the institutions in the 2009 sample. No meaningful patterns of statistical significance emerged with respect to workload and institutional type, control, or size. In regards to seminar type, a few isolated findings reached statistical significance. First, tenure-track faculty were more likely to teach academic seminars on various topics as part of their regular teaching load and less often taught extended orientation seminars within the scope of their regular job duties. Additionally, a significantly higher proportion of student affairs professionals taught preprofessional seminars and basic study skills seminars as part of their assigned responsibilities than other types of first-year seminars.

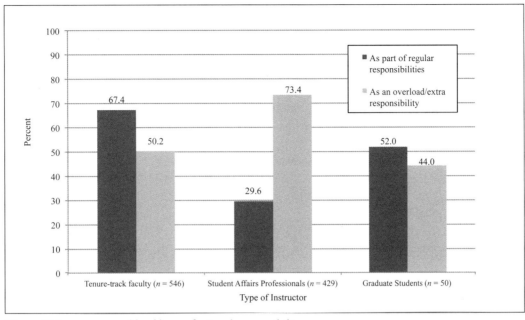

Figure 12. Instructor workload by professional responsibility.

A small percentage of respondents to the workload question indicated *other* instead of or in addition to the options of the workload being part of regular responsibilities or an overload. For both tenure-track faculty and student affairs professionals, the most common explanation of this *other* categorization of their first-year seminar teaching workload was described as some form of supplemental compensation, such as extra stipend or professional development funds, or as an adjunct or contract position. Further explanations included the first-year seminar teaching position falling into the catchall category of *additional duties* in a job description or as an entirely volunteer opportunity. Among the few responses pertaining to the open-ended *other* workload question for graduate students, volunteering was also a common response, which was further described as a valuable opportunity to get teaching experience on a volunteer basis or through a formalized practicum or internship opportunity.

As indicated by the *other* responses, compensation is tightly bound to the issue of workload. Therefore, the 2009 questionnaire contained a series of questions about remuneration for first-year seminar instruction. As shown in Table 15, a stipend was the most commonly reported form of payment for every type of first-year instructor and was, by far, the most significant form of compensation for adjunct faculty and graduate students. No compensation was the second most commonly reported category both as a component of their primary position description or in the form of volunteer work. Other forms of compensation, such as release time, professional development funds, and graduate student support, were used infrequently across all instructor categories. Given that both time and money are often overtaxed and limited resources, these data suggest that other compensation models may need to be examined as possibilities for first-year instructors.

Table 15

Type of Instructor Compensation by Professional Responsibility

Compensation	Adjunct faculty (n = 409)	Tenure-track (n = 546)	Student affairs (n = 429)	Other professional (n = 266)	Grad student (n = 50)
Stipend	52.6	37.2	46.9	44.4	54.0
None	13.7	35.7	34.5	33.5	36.0
Release time	2.0	5.1	5.4	4.1	n/a
Unrestricted professional development funds	1.5	2.6	1.9	1.5	n/a
Graduate student support	0.5	0.4	0.5	0.4	n/a
Other	35.2	29.1	22.1	28.6	26.0

Differences in compensation patterns emerged when these data were analyzed by institutional type and control. Most notably, four-year campuses more often used a stipend as seminar instructor compensation than their two-year institutional counterparts (Table 16). This finding was consistent for all professional categories of first-year seminar instructors and ranged from a 16.7 to 21.6 percentage-point difference. Similarly, private institutions offered stipends at a higher rate than public colleges and universities for all professional categories of first-year seminar instructors (Table 17). Differences ranged from 7 to 8 percentage points for adjunct and tenure-track faculty as well as other campus professionals and went as high as a 15.5 percentage-point difference for student affairs professionals at public and private campuses.

Table 16

Instructor Stipend by Institutional Type

Instructor role	Percent at four-year	Percent at two-year	Difference
Adjunct faculty (n = 409)	60.2	38.6	21.6**
Other campus professionals (n = 266)	48.6	28.6	20.0**
Student affairs professionals (n = 429)	51.1	34.0	17.1**
Tenure-track faculty (n = 546)	40.2	23.5	16.7**

**$p < 0.01$.

Table 17
Instructor Stipend by Institutional Control

Instructor role	Percent at private	Percent at public	Difference
Student affairs professionals ($n = 429$)	55.7	40.2	15.5**
Tenure-track faculty ($n = 546$)	41.4	32.7	8.7*
Other campus professionals ($n = 266$)	48.4	40.8	7.6
Adjunct faculty ($n = 409$)	57.1	49.8	7.3

*$p < 0.05$. **$p < 0.01$.

Since a stipend was the most commonly reported form of first-year instructor compensation across all categories of professional responsibility and was among the few categories of remuneration that yielded significant findings for analyses by institutional characteristics, it is interesting to look more closely at this type of compensation. The survey instrument included items that asked about the amount of the stipend per class for each professional category of seminar instructor on an 11-point scale ranging from *$500 or less* to *more than $4,000*. Table 18 shows the average amount of the first-year seminar instructor stipend for each professional category of instructor. Overall, these data indicate that the average amount of first-year seminar instructor stipend ranges between $1,001 to $2,000 per class for faculty (both tenure-track and adjunct) as well as for student affairs and other campus professionals. Graduate student instructors who receive stipends for first-year seminar instruction receive a slightly lower amount that averages between $501 and $1,000 per class. A calculation of mean stipend amounts by instructor role showed that adjunct faculty tend to receive the highest stipend. Tenure-track faculty and other campus professionals are nearly tied for the second and third positions and student affairs professionals represent the lowest paid category of first-year seminar instructors among professional roles (i.e., except graduate students). It is important to note, however, that stipend rates can be influenced by institutional payroll policies and collective bargaining agreements as well as the amount of credits the first-year seminar carries (i.e., one-credit seminars are likely to generate lower stipends than are three-credit courses). The notion that rates of pay and stipend amounts are complex issues is further supported by the high standard deviation for the mean in each category, thereby indicating that there is wide variation within each of these statistics.

Table 18
Average Amount of Instructor Compensation per Course by Professional Responsibility

Instructor role	M	SD
Adjunct faculty (*n* = 216)	3.82	2.11
Tenure-track faculty (*n* = 204)	3.41	2.12
Other campus professional (*n* = 119)	3.40	1.94
Student affairs professionals (*n* = 202)	3.06	1.65
Graduate student (*n* = 27)	2.70	2.39

Note. Response scale was 1: $500 or less; 2: $501-1,000; 3: $1,001-1,500; 4: $1,501-2,000; 5: $2,001-2,500; 6: $2,501-3,000; 7: $3,001-3,500; 8: 3,501-4,000; 9: 4,001-4,500; 10: $4,501-5,000; 11: more than $5,000.

One other analysis of disaggregated data for first-year seminar instructor compensation yielded statistically significant and consistent findings: the use of *other* compensation models. Specifically, two-year campuses in the sample were more likely to use other forms of compensation than stipends, graduate student support, release time, or unrestricted professional development funds (Table 19) by differences that ranged from 5.2 to 22.6 percentage points. Additionally, public institutions more often reported *other* compensation models than private colleges and universities, most notably for other campus professionals (Table 20).

Table 19
Other Instructor Compensation by Institutional Type

Instructor role	Percent at four-year	Percent at two-year	Difference
Other campus professionals (*n* = 266)	23.8	46.4	-22.6**
Adjunct faculty (*n* = 409)	28.0	48.3	-20.3**
Tenure-track faculty (*n* = 546)	25.9	43.9	-18.0**
Student affairs professionals (*n* = 429)	19.2	31.1	-5.2**

**$p < 0.01$.

Table 20
Other Instructor Compensation by Institutional Control

Instructor role	Percent at private	Percent at public	Difference
Other campus professionals (*n* = 266)	21.8	34.5	-12.7*
Tenure-track faculty (*n* = 546)	24.6	33.8	-9.2*
Student affairs professionals (*n* = 429)	17.3	25.8	-8.5*
Adjunct faculty (*n* = 409)	32.5	36.9	-4.4

*$p < 0.05$.

One would hope that the responses to the *other* category of the survey question regarding compensation would have provided several examples of innovative models for payment and rewards for first-year seminar instructors. The responses analyzed therein did not yield such findings. Overwhelmingly, feedback on this open-ended item provided detailed descriptions of monetary compensation models that respondents must have identified as outside of the *stipend* category of response. This was especially true for adjunct faculty (144 responses to the open-ended survey item), student affairs professionals (95 responses), and other campus professionals (76 responses) who often listed adjunct contracts, extra compensation agreements, hourly salary, and course pay rates in their open-ended answers to the *other* compensation question. In a few instances, respondents indicated that first-year seminar instruction was a part of regular job duties and, thus, did not garner additional remuneration, but there were very few models of innovative payment strategies in the responses for instructors. *Other* responses for tenure-track faculty (*n* = 158) were also dominated by additional information about pay structures that most notably fell into three categories: (a) additional payment (e.g., educational allowance, adjunct contract, hourly lecture rate); (b) expectation that it is part of their regular teaching load; or (c) overload. However, while few and far between, the responses to *other* compensation models for tenure-track faculty also yielded some innovative ideas regarding alternative reward and payments, such as

⬦ "Vita/portfolio line for tenure and promotion"
⬦ Departmental compensation (e.g., "direct transfer of funds to department to use for travel")
⬦ "After 3 years of teaching each semester, a paid semester leave"
⬦ "Release time"
⬦ Funds for research or professional development
⬦ Monetary support for "peer teaching assistant...travel funding for students in course"
⬦ "Stipend to develop the course [and] funds for activities outside the classroom"
⬦ Payment for faculty development and training
⬦ "Gift card at the end of the semester"

Instructor Training

As shown in Figure 13, approximately three quarters of responding institutions offered training for first-year seminar instructors, and half required it of their instructors. Four-year institutions both offered and required training of first-year instructors at a higher rate than two-year campuses in the sample by approximately 10 percentage points for both comparisons. There was also a slight curvilinear relationship between first-year class size and offering instructor training, whereby institutions with the smallest first-year classes (less than 1,000) and largest class sizes (greater than 4,000) were less likely to offer first-year instructor training than those institutions with class sizes in the 2,000-4,000-student range. One major difference emerged with respect to seminar type and required instructor training. Only 16.7% of institutions offering a primary preprofessional or discipline-linked seminar required instructor training, while over half of institutions reporting data on other first-year seminar types required training of their instructors.

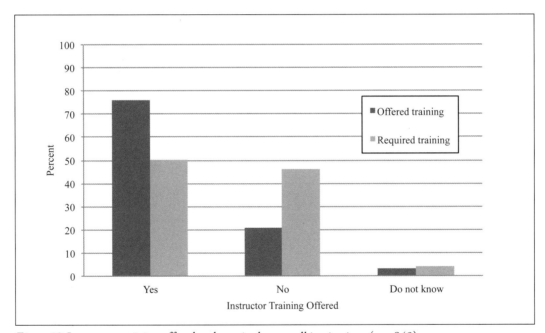

Figure 13. Instructor training offered and required across all institutions ($n = 849$).

Survey responses indicate that the format of first-year seminar instructor training tends to be shorter, one-shot training sessions. More than half of respondents reported that instructor training is a day or less in duration (Figure 14). Further, first-year instructor training at two-year colleges tended to be shorter than at four-year institutions with greater than 70% reporting that such training is a day or less. However, it is interesting to note that of the 136 open-ended answers to the *other* category for the question about duration of instructor training, approximately half ($n = 67$) clearly indicated training formats that were longer than one week. The most popular format of these longer training options was an intense training session ranging from a half-day to a multiday workshop or retreat followed by ongoing training throughout the term that the instructor was teaching. Most commonly, these ongoing training opportunities take the form of faculty meetings, workshops, or in-service opportunities. However, analyses of open-ended data also reveal some instances of one-on-one mentoring of instructors, especially those who are new or graduate students, by experienced seminar instructors, seminar leadership, or staff of teaching and learning centers on campuses in the sample.

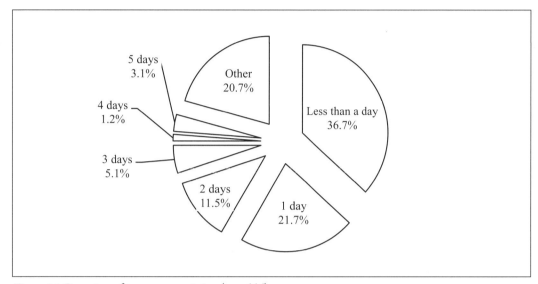

Figure 14. Duration of instructor training ($n = 646$).

Course Practices

One of the criteria for excellence in first-year experience programs is that they should represent comprehensive and integrated approaches to the support of new students (Barefoot et al., 2005). While it is a common mistake for people to call first-year seminars, *the first-year experience*, seminars are, in fact, only one of a number of tactics that are commonly used to support first-year students. However, seminars often provide the platform for creating connections among multiple programs and initiatives to support the transition and success of first-year students. As such, the Survey included several questions to collect multi-institutional data on four first-year initiatives or programmatic efforts commonly found in first-year seminars: online components, service-learning, linked courses (i.e., learning communities), and common reading. The 2009 Survey not only included quantitative measures for these four course practices (Table 21) but also gathered more descriptive data about the first three via open-ended survey items.

Table 21
First-Year Initiatives Associated With First-Year Seminars (n = 848)

First-year initiative	Percent
Online components	52.9
Service-learning	40.3
Linked courses (i.e., learning communities)	35.7
Common reading	31.0

Online Components

As shown in Table 21, more than half of the survey respondents indicated that their primary type of first-year seminar incorporated an online component. While there was no difference in the use of an online component by type of first-year seminar, statistically significant ($p < 0.01$) differences emerged for several institutional characteristics. Specifically, two-year campuses used online components in first-year seminars more frequently than four-year institutions (61.6% vs. 49.8%) as did public institutions when compared to their private counterparts in the sample (62.3% compared to 42.8%). Institutions with first-year class sizes less than 500 (44.7%) and between 1,001 and 2,000 students (48.0%) were significantly ($p < 0.01$) below the overall average (52.9%) with respect to the integration of online instruction. Additional data analysis suggest that online components may be used as a way to achieve economy of scale as larger institutions tended to use them slightly more frequently than campuses with smaller first-year classes ($r = 0.09$, $p < 0.01$).

Approximately 15% of respondents also indicate that their institutions offer sections of the first-year seminar entirely online. Similar to the data on incorporating online elements, online-only sections were significantly more likely ($p < 0.01$) in two-year colleges (32.9%) and public institutions (21.9%). The relationship with size of the first-year class was less linear, with online-only first-year seminars being offered most frequently among institutions with first-year classes between 2,001 and 3,000 and those over 4,000.

Respondents from 441 institutions provided written feedback to the open-ended survey item asking *describe the online components that are included in the course,* thereby, providing a very comprehensive view of the use of online technologies in first-year seminars. Overwhelmingly, the most common use of technology in the first-year seminar is via a course management system that is often used as the repository for course documents, a portal for the submission of assignments, and course communication (Skipper & Keup, 2010). Another common web-based seminar component was the use of online tutorials and assessments, such as ones related to alcohol or substance use and abuse, information literacy, and awareness of campus resources. Interestingly, while social media is certainly a growing part of first-year students' lives, it does not seem to have permeated these classes; only a handful of respondents mentioned social networking sites in their toolbox of online seminar components. A minority of institutions are using information technology in more innovative ways, including online textbooks, e-portfolios, and online communication, such as "blogs, wikis, listservs, and the creation of web pages or other online projects." In an example of the use of multiple online components, one institution provided Mac notebooks to all students and Apple training to all instructors on iMovie. Using these tools and training, "students use the

Internet in classrooms as part of directed projects," and "numerous sections have Skyped or used iChat as major components in the classroom." Save for these few examples, the use of online components in first-year seminars seems limited to course management and class organization and less focused on innovative pedagogy.

Service-Learning

Incorporating service-learning elements into the traditional classroom have proven to enhance students' development across course application, awareness of civic problems, and classroom performance (Markus, Howard, & King, 1993). Survey respondents indicated that 40.3% of seminars include a service-learning component (Table 21), nearly identical to the respondents of the 2006 Survey (40.2%). Further analyses of these responses showed that four-year campuses in the sample were significantly ($p < 0.01$) more likely to use service-learning in first-year seminars than two-year colleges (35.9% vs. 19.6%), but there were no statistically significant differences by institutional control or size of the first-year class. When reports of using service-learning were disaggregated by type of first-year seminar, statistically significant differences ($p < 0.01$) emerged (Figure 15). Most notably, institutions reporting an academic seminar on various topics as a primary type incorporated service-learning at the highest rate followed closely by institutions with hybrid seminars. Conversely, institutions that had extended orientation and basic study skills seminars were least likely to use service-learning in their classes.

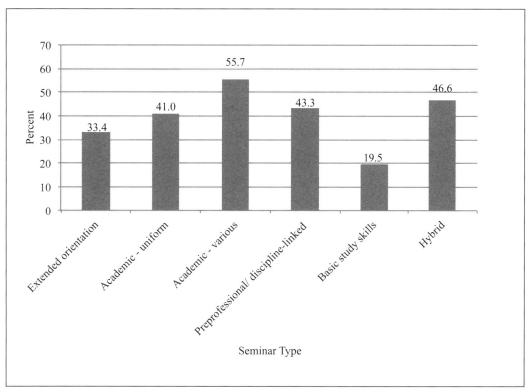

Figure 15. Seminar included service-learning component by seminar type (*n* = 848).

Again, the 331 responses to the open-ended item invited survey respondents to provide additional detail regarding the use of this pedagogical technique. As with many aspects of first-year seminars, there was significant variation both within as well as between institutions with respect to the focus and use of service-learning in the course. Service-learning experiences were often connected to a specific theme for the first-year seminar overall or within each section. Despite such variation, survey responses show some commonality to these service-learning experiences. Most notably, the service tends to be rather short in duration, usually less than 10 hours (Skipper & Keup, 2010). Further, service is most often structured as a one-time experience rather than ongoing involvement. Also, while a minority of institutions mentioned first-year seminar students' involvement in the development or organization of the service-learning experience, most were either prescribed service activities or students were allowed to select from existing campus service opportunities. Finally, homelessness, hunger, and at-risk youth are common foci of service activities among the institutions that provided the topics or themes of their service-learning activity (Skipper & Keup).

While not explicitly stated in the wording of the survey item, service-learning goes beyond just engaging in or requiring a service activity of students. True service-learning is an integrated component of the course, reinforces course objectives and learning outcomes, and includes a reflective component as part of the experience in the course (Zlotkowski, 2002, 2005). Several of the open-ended survey responses paid heed to reflection as an important aspect of service-learning. Specifically, many institutional representatives responding to the Survey included references to reflection activities related to the service experience, such as written papers, presentations, class discussions, and journals (Skipper & Keup, 2010).

Linked Courses or Learning Communities

As a form of integrative learning, first-year seminars are often paired or linked with other courses or programs. These linked courses (i.e., learning communities) provide students a more collaborative learning experience in which interdisciplinary subject mastery is encouraged (Tinto, 1998). More than one third (35.7%) of participating institutions reported having sections linked to one or more courses. Public institutions (45.4%) were significantly more likely ($p < 0.01$) than private institutions (25.4%) to link the seminar into a learning community. The likelihood of the seminar being linked within a learning community significantly increased ($p < 0.01$) as size of the first-year class increased, ranging from 23.2% for first-year classes less than 500 to 67.2% for classes larger than 4,001. The practice of linking other course(s) with a first-year seminar did not differ significantly by seminar type, institutional control, or two- or four-year campuses.

Approximately 300 institutions in the sample responded affirmatively to the survey item that asked, *Are any sections linked to one or more other courses (i.e., "learning community" – enrolling a cohort of students into two or more courses),* and 286 provided additional open-ended data to describe the linked-course (i.e., learning community) component of their first-year experience. The wide range of open-ended responses for this item provided further support for the complexity of purpose, use, and structure of linked courses with respect to first-year seminars. Linked-course structures (i.e., learning communities) serve a variety of student populations and needs at the respondent institutions, such as

◇ Establishing support for academically at-risk populations
◇ Presenting interventions for groups of students in the same major
◇ Providing organized cocurricular and social experiences for new students
◇ Offering living-learning communities for residential students
◇ Formalizing campus support structures for commuter and/or adult students

◇ Creating a network for honors students
◇ Building a foundation for student interests around a theme as with freshman interest groups (FIGs)

Despite these differences, many first-year seminars were linked to developmental courses (e.g., English, reading, math), which tend to have a history of a high failure or withdrawal rates among first-year students, and general education requirements, most notably first-year composition (Skipper & Keup, 2010).

Finally, these open-ended data yielded rich descriptions of highly integrated, learning communities that focused on thoughtfully selected thematic links and interdisciplinary explorations. However, many other examples represented structures that were little more than co-enrollment models for first-year seminars and other courses (Skipper & Keup, 2010). Such differences in purpose and student populations allow learning communities within first-year seminars to be a flexible pedagogical tool. This variation in the degree of meaningful connection between linked courses suggests that institutions and the first-year students they serve may not be gaining the full benefit of learning communities as an integrated, intentional learning experience.

Common Reading

Often recognized as another formal mechanism to integrate students into the first-year experience and interdisciplinary coursework, roughly one third (31.0%) of survey respondents reported that a component of the seminar was a first-year or summer reading program. Four-year institutions (38.2%) and private institutions (35.4%) were significantly more likely ($p < 0.01$) to incorporate a reading program into the seminar compared to community colleges (10.5%) and public institutions (26.9%), respectively. No significant differences existed across institutional size or seminar type.

Conclusion

While results from the 2009 administration of the National Survey of First-Year Seminars identify statistically significant differences in instruction and pedagogy by institutional characteristics and seminar type, they also reveal a prevailing portrait of the professional role of instructors, compensation for teaching, and instructor training. For instance, the instruction of these courses tends to be dominated by full-time faculty (both tenure-track and non-tenure-track), although instructors with other professional responsibilities, such as student affairs professionals, and adjunct faculty also teach in these seminars. Stipend, adjunct contract, or some form of additional instructor compensation was the prominent form of payment for teaching first-year seminars. More innovative remuneration models (e.g., release time, professional development funds and experiences, graduate student support) are significantly underrepresented. Finally, first-year seminar instructor preparation is generally structured as a shorter, one-shot training session with many institutions providing additional instructor development and ongoing support throughout the term that the instructor is teaching.

Between one third and one half of survey respondents indicated using various course practices (i.e., online components, service-learning, linked courses, and common reading) in combination with first-year seminars. Similar to instruction, these practices are often used in a more functional rather than novel approaches (e.g., online components consisting of course management systems, merely linking courses for learning communities, one-shot service-learning experiences). It seems that these course practices have great, albeit currently unrealized, potential for transformation into truly high-impact learning experiences for students and valuable complements to a first-year seminar as pillars in an integrated, intentional first-year experience.

Assessing the Seminar

With every educational initiative, assessment is a valuable means of gathering information and feedback for the purposes of "measuring effectiveness, accountability, and improvement" (Schuh, 2005, p. 144). First-year seminars are no exception, and a hallmark of high-quality seminars is ongoing assessment that guides decisions regarding the content, instruction, and administration of this important curricular intervention (Jewler, 1989; Schuh, 2005; Swing, 2001; Upcraft, 2005). This section provides a summary of responses to the bank of questions on the 2009 National Survey of First-Year Seminars covering assessment practices. The highlighted findings will offer statistical evidence regarding first-year seminar objectives, as well as common assessment methods and outcomes for these courses. Finally, an overview is provided of the open-ended responses from institutional representatives about the findings from their assessment of first-year seminars.

More than half (56.5%) of the institutions that reported they offered a first-year seminar on the 2009 Survey also indicated that they had formally assessed or evaluated the seminar since fall 2006 (the year of the last National Survey administration). Conversely, approximately one third of the respondents shared that they had not engaged in any such formal assessment process for their seminar in the past three years. Interestingly, nearly 10% reported that they did not know whether assessment activities had taken place in that time frame, thus serving as evidence that first-year seminar assessment has yet to fully engage all stakeholders at these participating institutions. Further evidence of the need for assessment at these colleges and universities can be found from the open-ended responses to the survey item that asked respondents to *describe the most significant findings from your assessment and evaluation of first-year seminar outcomes*. Twenty-five of the 365 written responses referenced the need for assessment or the desire to acquire the results of evaluation processes currently underway.

Course Objectives

For most assessment processes to be effective, they must clearly identify the purpose and goals of the initiative (Huba & Freed, 2000; Maki, 2004; Upcraft, Crissman Ishler, & Swing, 2005). Much like "a journey without a destination likely leads to aimless wandering..., without identifying the desired outcomes of...a first-year seminar, the course is likely to lack curricular cohesiveness and impact" (Keup & Petschauer, 2011, p. 38). Although the statistics for the items related to course objectives on the 2009 Survey were covered in detail earlier in this report, a review of these findings is necessary to provide a foundation for survey results regarding assessment. Table 22 summarizes the responses to the survey item that requested institutional representatives to *select the three most important course objectives for the first-year seminar*. Overall, developing academic skills, developing a connection with the institution, and providing an orientation to campus resources and services were of the highest priority to institutions. Conversely, fewer than 10% of respondents indicated that introduction to a discipline, the development of financial literacy, and the encouragement of arts participation were of similar importance with respect to first-year seminar objectives.

Table 22
Most Important Course Objectives (n = 890)

Outcome	Percent
Develop academic skills	54.6
Develop a connection with the institution	50.2
Provide orientation to campus resources and services	47.6
Self-exploration/personal development	28.5
Create common first-year experience	23.3
Develop support network/friendships	17.4
Increase student/faculty interaction	16.9
Improve sophomore return rates	15.5
Develop writing skills	11.9
Introduce a discipline	7.0
Develop financial literacy	1.1
Encourage arts participation	0.6
Other (please specify)	8.1

Note. Percentages will sum to more than 100% because respondents were allowed to mark more than one category.

Seventy-two institutional representatives chose to add to the list of first-year seminar objectives via the open-ended response to the *other* category. In several instances, this response field was used to articulate an institutional or seminar mission statement or course objective that incorporated several of the outcomes as with the campus that replied that the objective of their first-year seminar was to "(1) recognize responsibilities as students and practice those behaviors; (2) identify characteristics of successful students, barriers to college success, and strategies for success; and (3) establish relationships with peers, faculty, and staff." There were also several open-ended entries that articulated additional course objectives for first-year seminars in the 2009 sample. The two most common additions highlighted in these responses were the development of critical thinking or analytical skills and the introduction of the liberal arts. One institution stated in their written response that an important seminar objective was to "develop a comprehensive understanding of the liberal arts and engage in substantive academic work to develop critical/comprehensive learning skills." Other common entries in the open-ended field for important first-year seminar objectives included

◇ Major exploration, preprofessional preparation, and career development
◇ Development of study skills
◇ Institutional mission introduction
◇ Improvement of information literacy and fluency
◇ Development of oral communication skills

As with all items on the 2009 Survey, these data were disaggregated by institutional type, control, and size (as measured by first-year class size) as well as by first-year seminar type. Again in the summary of findings highlighted earlier, the analyses of responses regarding first-year seminar objectives yielded statistically significant findings for several of these subgroup analyses.

Significant Course Objectives Findings Across Institutional Type

◇ Both two-year and four-year campuses in the sample indicated that *develop academic skills* (57.0% and 53.7%, respectively) and *develop a connection with the institution* (51.5% and 49.8%) were important course objectives.

◇ The greatest difference between two- and four-year institutions was with respect to the outcome *provide orientation to campus resources and services* with two-year campuses ranking this among their top three outcomes at a rate that was 25.5 percentage points ($p < 0.01$) higher than four-year colleges and universities.

◇ Other outcomes that yielded statistically significant higher rankings among two-year campuses than four-year institutions were *self-exploration/personal development* (11.5 percentage-point difference, $p < 0.01$) and *develop financial literacy* (2.5 percentage-point difference, $p < 0.01$).

◇ Conversely, four-year campuses prioritized several course objectives higher than their two-year counterparts, including *increase student/faculty interaction* (14.8 percentage-point difference, $p < 0.01$); *create common first-year experience* (11.4 percentage-point difference, $p < 0.01$); *develop writing skills* (7.5 percentage-point difference, $p < 0.01$); and *introduce a discipline* (6.6 percentage-point difference, $p < 0.01$).

Significant Course Objectives Findings Across Institutional Control

◇ Similar to the analysis by institutional type, both public and private institutions reported that *develop academic skills* (58.2% and 50.7%, respectively) and *develop a connection with the institution* (51.9% and 48.4%, respectively) were among the most important outcomes for the first-year seminar.

◇ Three course objectives were ranked higher among public institutions than private colleges at a statistically significant level: *provide orientation to campus resources and services* (17.1 percentage-point difference, $p < 0.01$); *develop academic skills* (7.5 percentage-point difference, $p < 0.05$); and *develop financial literacy* (1.7 percentage-point difference $p < 0.05$).

◇ Private institutions ranked the following seminar objectives among the top three more frequently than public campuses in the sample at a statistically significant level ($p < 0.01$): *develop writing skills* (12.7 percentage-point difference); *create common first-year experience* (12.1 percentage-point difference); and *increase student/faculty interaction* (8.2 percentage-point difference).

Significant Course Objectives Findings Across Seminar Type

◇ *Develop a connection with the institution, develop academic skills*, and *provide orientation to campus resources and services* were rated as important course objectives for all seminar types (i.e., extended orientation, academic with uniform content, academic on various topics, preprofessional or discipline-linked, basic study skills, and hybrid seminars).

◇ Survey respondents who identified academic seminars on various topics as their primary seminar type also selected *increase student/faculty interaction* as an important course objective while other types did not prioritize this outcome as highly.

◇ Institutions that reported a preprofessional or discipline-linked seminar as their primary type were also more likely to identify *introduce a discipline* as an important course objective than other seminar types.

These data confirmed the subtle differences by institution and seminar type. However, as reported earlier, overwhelming evidence suggests that all institutions—no matter their institutional type, control, or size—significantly value (a) developing a connection with the institution, (b) developing academic skills, and (c) providing an orientation to various campus resources and services as important course objectives.

Assessment Methods

After the goals of the first-year seminar have been identified and articulated via the course objectives, "institutions must design methods for assessing the seminar's effectiveness in these areas" (Tobolowsky & Associates, 2008, p. 87). The Survey included several items to collect data about the decisions that comprise institutional assessment of first-year seminars, including use of qualitative and quantitative methodologies, selection of local and national survey instruments, and specific outcomes of interest in the assessment process.

Survey responses indicated that quantitative assessment strategies are employed more frequently for first-year assessment. Most notably, the use of student course evaluations was nearly universal among institutions participating in the 2009 National Survey (Table 23). Additionally, approximately three quarters of respondents reported that they used survey instruments and analyses of institutional data in their assessment processes for the course. Interestingly, these assessment practices yielded very few statistically significant differences when analyzed by institutional characteristics or seminar type thus suggesting that course evaluations, survey instruments, and analyses of institutional data are becoming fixtures as assessment methods for first-year seminars across all colleges and universities.

While not used as frequently as quantitative assessment methods, many institutions in the sample responded that they also employed qualitative strategies in their first-year seminar assessment process (Table 23). In fact, it appears that these assessment methodologies are a primary means by which first-year seminar instructors are included in the assessment of these courses. More specifically, both focus groups and individual interviews are used more often with instructors than with students although both are also used to generate student feedback about the course as well. Similar to the disaggregated analyses of quantitative methods, comparisons of qualitative assessment methodologies between institutional type, control, and size generated only a few statistically significant differences. Most notably, private institutions used focus groups with instructors at a slightly higher rate than public colleges and universities ($p < 0.01$), and institutions that reported academic seminars with uniform content as their primary seminar type used focus groups with both students and instructors more frequently ($p < 0.05$) than other institutions.

Table 23
First-Year Seminar Assessment Methods (n = 475)

	Percent
Quantitative assessment strategies	
Student course evaluation	94.9
Survey instrument	75.3
Analysis of institutional data	75.3
Qualitative assessment strategies	
Focus groups with instructors	51.3
Individual interviews with instructors	45.6
Focus groups with students	42.6
Individual interviews with students	30.2

Note. Percentages will sum to more than 100% because respondents were allowed to mark more than one category.

As shown in Table 23, survey instruments were tied as the second most common assessment method. Yet this summary statistic tends to oversimplify the myriad of different options embedded within the *survey instrument* category. Over the past few decades, there has been an increased demand for accountability in higher education that has created an industry around the development and administration of survey instruments as well as analysis of the data that are generated from them. As such, there are a number of national assessment tools for purchase as off-the-shelf instruments as well as a wide range of software and web-based services to assist in the design and data collection for institutionally developed surveys. In order to capture current information about these decisions, the Survey included items about the types of surveys being used to assess first-year seminars at respondent institutions.

Of the 357 participating institutions that reported that using a survey for first-year seminar assessment, 84% reported that the instrument was locally developed, which represented the most popular option. However, more than half (52.4%) of these same respondents indicated that a national survey was used to assess the seminar, a practice that was even more common among the four-year institutions in the sample (17.0 percentage point difference over two-year campuses, $p < 0.01$). A follow-up question inquired as to the specific national survey instrument used, which showed that the National Survey of Student Engagement (NSSE) was, by far, the most popular national assessment tool for first-year seminars among participating institutions (Figure 16). Approximately one third of the institutions in the sample used the Freshman Survey sponsored by the Cooperative Institutional Research Program (CIRP), but a much smaller proportion used the CIRP follow-up survey, Your First College Year (YFCY).

More than 20.0% (*n* = 39) of the sample indicated that they used another instrument not listed among the response options on the survey item. Open-ended responses show that institutions are using several other surveys administered through the Center for Postsecondary Research (the home of NSSE), such as the Beginning College Survey of Student Engagement (BCSSE), Faculty Survey of Student Engagement (FSSE), College Student Experiences Survey (CSEQ), and the Survey of Entering Student Engagement (SENSE). Other surveys by Educational Benchmarking Incorporated (EBI), the sponsor of the First-Year Initiative (FYI) Survey, were mentioned in eight open-ended respondents. Additional national survey instruments identified by more than one institution in the open-ended responses include the Individual Development and Educational Assessment (IDEA), the Student Satisfaction Inventory (SSI), the Collegiate Learning Assessment (CLA), and the Foundations of Excellence Surveys sponsored by the John N. Gardner Institute for Excellence in Undergraduate Education.

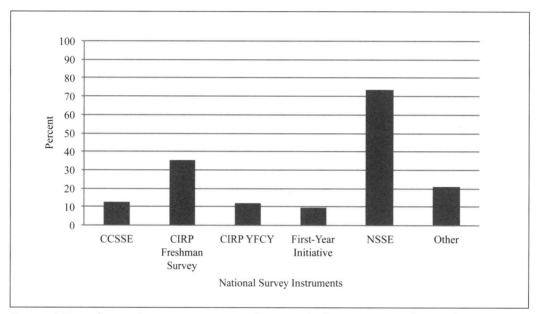

Figure 16. Type of national survey instrument used to assess the first-year seminar ($n = 187$).

Assessment Outcomes

The Survey also inquired as to the outcomes that were measured via these assessment methodologies.[6] As shown in Table 24, persistence to the second year of college and satisfaction, both with the faculty and institution, were at the top of the list of assessment outcomes followed by academic

---

[6] A limitation of the survey administration and analysis was the way that the assessment item measure was included in the online questionnaire. The item was worded *Select each outcome that was measured (check all that apply)* and provided 11 response options including an *other, please describe* option with a text box. This item was intended to be an option for all survey respondents who indicated that the primary first-year seminar on their campus had been assessed or evaluated since fall 2006. However, due to an error in survey construction, the assessment outcome question was structured such that only those survey participants who indicated that they conducted an assessment or evaluation via *analysis of institutional data* were provided the survey item on assessment outcomes. Therefore, only 357 of the total 475 eligible respondents (75%) for this item were allowed the option to submit data on first-year seminar assessment outcomes, which may limit the generalizability and interpretation of these data.

performance, use of campus services, connection with peers, and participation in campus activities. Sixty-six institutional respondents identified *other* assessment outcomes, including

◇ Writing ability
◇ Satisfaction with the course
◇ Achievement of learning or course outcomes
◇ Student self-reports of improvement and course impact
◇ Satisfaction with advising
◇ Civic engagement and involvement in service
◇ Students' understanding of specific aspects of institutional identity and culture
◇ Critical thinking

Table 24
First-Year Seminar Assessment Outcomes (n = 357)

Outcome	Percent
Persistence to sophomore year	73.7
Satisfaction with faculty	70.9
Satisfaction with the institution	65.3
Grade-point average	58.0
Use of campus services	51.0
Connections with peers	49.3
Participation in campus activities	49.0
Out-of-class student/faculty interaction	47.1
Academic abilities	42.0
Persistence to graduation	38.4
Other	18.5

Although the responses to this survey item were not written to parallel those listed for the item on seminar objectives, it is interesting to observe the differences in outcomes that were highly measured and those that were named as top objectives. Most notably, almost three quarters of survey respondents reported that they measured first-to-second-year persistence as an outcome of first-year seminars, but only 15.5% of respondents identified this measure as one of their three most important course objectives (see Table 22, p. 50). In addition, more than 70% of institutions participating in the 2009 National Survey measured satisfaction with faculty as a seminar outcome, yet only 17% prioritized *increase student/faculty interaction* among their top course objectives. Similarly, there is a 15.1 percentage-point gap between the proportion of survey respondents who measured *satisfaction with the institution* as a first-year seminar outcome (65.3%) and the percent who reported *develop a connection with the institution* was an important course objective (50.2%). In order to truly inform the relevance and excellence of the first-year seminar, it is critical that assessment outcomes measure the stated objectives of the course. While not conclusive evidence, the statistics generated by the 2009 National Survey suggest institutional overreliance upon easily acquired assessment outcomes, such as retention rates and satisfaction measures, regardless of their alignment with stated goals of the seminar.

Assessment outcomes were reported consistently across all first-year seminar types. However, when survey data on assessment outcomes are analyzed by institutional characteristics, several statistically significant differences emerge. As shown in Table 25, four-year institutions identified connections with peers and faculty; satisfaction with faculty and the institution; first-to-second-year persistence, and participation in campus activities as assessment outcomes at a higher rate than two-year institutions in the sample. In addition, public institutions shared that persistence measures, both to the sophomore year and to graduation, and grade point averages were among their first-year seminar assessment outcomes more often than private colleges and universities (Table 26).

Table 25
First-Year Seminar Assessment Outcomes by Institutional Type (n = 357)

Outcome	Two-year	Four-year	Difference
Percentages larger for two-year			
Other	23.9	17.1	6.8
Percentages larger for four-year			
Connections with peers	31.0	53.8	-22.8**
Out-of-class student/faculty interaction	29.6	51.4	-21.8**
Satisfaction with faculty	53.5	75.2	-21.7*
Satisfaction with the institution	47.9	69.6	-21.7*
Persistence to sophomore year	57.7	77.6	-19.9*
Participation in campus activities	35.2	52.4	-17.2*
Use of campus services	42.3	53.1	-10.8
Persistence to graduation	36.6	38.8	-2.2
Academic abilities	40.8	42.3	-1.5
Grade point average	57.2	57.7	-0.5

*$p < 0.05$. **$p < 0.01$.

Table 26
First-Year Seminar Assessment Outcomes by Institutional Affiliation (n = 357)

Outcome	Public	Private	Difference
Percentages larger for public			
Grade point average	66.7	49.2	17.5**
Persistence to sophomore year	80.0	67.2	12.8**
Persistence to graduation	44.4	32.2	12.2**
Other (please specify)	20.6	16.4	4.2
Academic abilities	43.3	40.7	2.6
Use of campus services	51.7	50.3	1.4
Participation in campus activities	49.4	48.6	0.8
Percentages larger for private			
Satisfaction with the institution	56.7	74.0	-17.3
Connections with peers	43.3	55.4	-12.1
Satisfaction with faculty	67.8	74.0	-6.2
Out-of-class student/faculty interaction	45.0	49.2	-4.2

**$p < 0.01$.

Only two assessment outcomes showed any statistically significant ($p < 0.01$) differences across the categories of size for the first-year class (Figure 17). Both *grade point average* and *persistence to sophomore year* tended to be more frequently reported by institutions with larger first-year student bodies with only a slight drop off for campuses with more than 4,000 first-year students.

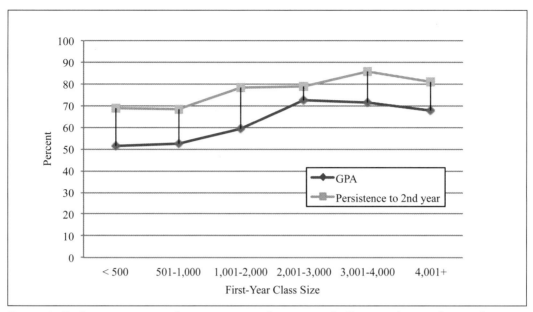

Figure 17. Grade point average and persistence to sophomore year by first-year class size (*n* = 357).

Assessment Findings

The 2009 National Survey of First-Year Seminars differed from previous iterations of the Survey in its introduction of a new item related to assessment findings. The 2009 Survey included an open-ended item that asked survey respondents to *describe the most significant findings from your assessment and evaluation of first-year seminar outcomes.* Therefore, institutional representatives were allowed to articulate these assessment results without limitation or prescription. Of the 475 survey participants who indicated that their institution had conducted an assessment of their primary first-year seminar in the previous three years, 365 provided an account of their first-year seminar assessment findings.

The open-ended responses were reviewed and coded by theme. Initially the response options for the survey questions related to course objectives (12 specific items, not including *other*, listed in Table 22, p. 50) and course outcomes (10 specific items, not including *other*, listed in Table 24, p. 55) were combined and collapsed to create 16 unique codes, which created the foundation for the analysis of survey responses about first-year assessment findings. Throughout the qualitative analysis, existing codes were expanded, combined, and in one instance (for *development of financial literacy*), deleted for lack of responses coded under this category. Further, 15 new codes were added to the scheme. The final result was a collection of 30 different categories of assessment findings, which are summarized in Table 27 along with the number of instances they were mentioned in the open-ended responses.

Table 27
First-Year Seminar Assessment Findings for All Institutions (n = 365)

Findings	Count[a]
Improved persistence and retention[b c]	112
Recommendations & action items for course improvement	73
Student satisfaction with course/useful course overall	67
Increased grade point average or academic performance[b]	40
Develop academic abilities, skills, and engagement[b c]	38
Feedback on students' preferred instructional techniques, method, & content	38
Increased student/faculty interaction[b c]	35
Negative, questionable, or no effects	29
Greater knowledge and use of campus services & resources[b c]	29
Academic & social interactions with peers[b c]	26
Assessment in process or needed (no assessment findings)	25
Development of a connection with the institution[c]	24
Student satisfaction with support for transition	17
Faculty/instructor satisfaction with course	13
Student satisfaction with peer mentor	12
Success of special student population (e.g., minority, commuter, first-generation)	12
Development of writing skills[c]	11
Successful pursuit of stated learning or course objectives and outcomes	11
Student satisfaction with institution[b]	10
Student satisfaction with advising	10
Participation in campus activities[b]	9
Broader view of education and/or world	9
Student satisfaction with faculty[b]	7
Favorable measurement or comparison on national assessment tool (e.g., NSSE, EBI, CLA)	7
Enhanced self-exploration or personal development[c]	5
Major and degree exploration	4
Introduction to a discipline[c]	3
Created a common first-year experience[c]	2
Arts participation[c]	1
Other	33

[a] The count does not represent unique institutions. Given the open-ended nature of the survey item, respondents could have reported more than one finding, which would then be coded across multiple categories.
[b] Indicates a code drawn from response options to survey item, *Select each outcome that was measured.*
[c] Indicates a code drawn from response options to survey item, *Select the three most important course objectives for the first-year seminar.*

By far, the assessment categories most often cited in the open-ended responses were increases in persistence and retention measures for first-year seminar participants, whether they were to the second term, the sophomore year, graduation, all three metrics, or without specific parameters. Other outcomes that were among the response options to the survey item summarized in Table 24 (p. 55) were also frequently reported in the open-ended data on first-year assessment findings. Increased academic performance, most often noted by higher grade point averages, was mentioned in 40 entries to the open-ended item. On a related note, the development of academic abilities, skills, and engagement was cited as among the most significant categories from first-year seminar participation for 38 survey respondents. This finding is illustrated by the institutional representative who shared "as a result of participation in the seminar, students report skill development in project and team management, presentation skills, critical thinking, accepting critical feedback from others, having confidence to speak to individuals in positions of power, assuming leadership positions in a team, and presenting oneself professionally."

Interestingly, institutions reporting assessment findings for both academic performance and development occasionally cited improvement on scores or benchmarks for specific national surveys, such as the NSSE or EBI, which was captured in a new code in the qualitative analysis represented in Table 27. A handful of other responses about the development of specific academic abilities were captured in other codes within the schema, most notably, the development of writing skills, which was identified as a significant category of assessment findings for 11 survey respondents. In fact, results of first-year seminar assessments not only showed development in writing ("many FYS faculty report significant improvement in organization, structure, and support of arguments in student writing") but also helped debunk the negative impressions that faculty may hold about students' writing abilities ("students are more proficient at writing than many faculty assume"). Finally, another new category of first-year seminar findings was related to success as measured by retention, academic performance, *and* academic development: the beneficial effect of first-year seminars on the success of specific student subpopulations, including historically underrepresented racial and ethnic groups, first-generation college students, and commuter students.

Perhaps these first-year seminar assessment results are related to interaction and satisfaction with faculty—often a defining feature of first-year seminars—which proved to be a significant category of first-year assessment results. More specifically, 35 respondents identified increased student/faculty interaction, most often within the course but sometimes outside the classroom, as an important result, making it seventh in the rank order of categories of first-year seminar assessment findings. Interestingly, student satisfaction with the faculty was not identified as frequently as increased student/faculty interactions in the report of assessment findings. However, increased student/faculty interactions were noted as a significant first-year seminar assessment category more frequently than the development of peer networks (*academic and social interactions with peers* in Table 27).

Student expressions of overall satisfaction with the seminar also dominated the open-ended responses and ranked third in the list of most commonly identified significant categories of first-year seminar assessment. In addition to student expressions that the course was beneficial, analyses of open-ended data yielded a new code related to faculty members' satisfaction with the course. Open-ended responses to this effect ranged from "both students and faculty applauded the program and its goals" to more specific mention of the faculty experience as instructors of the course, such as the institutional respondent who reported that "faculty find teaching the course a challenging experience that most seem to enjoy." Further, assessment feedback on faculty satisfaction with the course also suggests that the first-year seminar serves as a laboratory for testing pedagogy and new teaching techniques as with the respondent that indicated that "FYS faculty report a high level of using new ideas in their seminars, or taking ideas from their seminars and trying them in other classes."

Not all assessment feedback on the first-year seminar was uniformly positive. In fact, three new codes that arose in the analyses of open-ended responses showed the potential for improvement in the course on the respondent campuses. First, 73 responses to the survey item about significant findings from assessment and evaluation of first-year seminar outcomes identified recommendations for improvement and even outlined specific action steps to integrate these improvements in the future. In many instances, these recommendations related to the structure of the course, including the duration, grading, size, or application of credit for the course. In other examples, additional faculty training was planned; course objectives needed adjustment; and support materials for the course, including textbooks, were going to be re-examined. Second, the analysis of seminar assessment findings collected feedback about first-year students' preferred instructional techniques (e.g., greater reflection, links to learning communities, creative and interactive pedagogy) and course content (e.g., writing instruction, test-taking strategies, disciplinary links), which many respondents indicated would be considered for future sections. Third, 29 respondents indicated that their assessment and evaluation efforts yielded no results or negative results with respect to their outcomes of interest, most often retention and student dissatisfaction with the course. In several of these instances, respondents also indicated that further analyses were being conducted to confirm these findings and/or the course was under revision to address these assessment results. The value of such critical feedback is illustrated by the respondent who shared,

> although students tend to not want to come [to class] (they don't receive credit), the general comments in the student evaluations indicate that they recognize its value and they have learned a lot [sic] once the 8 week sessions are over. Students provide good feedback on what they would like to see changed; [in] following years these recommendations are addressed as the syllabi and course planning instruments are reevaluated.

It is perhaps not surprising that retention, academic performance and development, and interaction with faculty and peers were within the top 10 most frequently cited first-year seminar assessment findings. However, other outcomes typically associated with first-year seminars were not as commonly identified in the open-ended responses. For example, the development of a connection with the institution and student satisfaction with support for the transition fell just below the top 10 threshold, and participation in campus activities, personal exploration, and the creation of a common first-year experience were all mentioned by fewer than 10 respondents as significant first-year seminar assessment findings. It appears that respondents to the 2009 Survey valued assessment results related to more generalized metrics of success or, conversely, very specific findings for the course. However, open-ended responses also revealed other outcomes of significance to first-year seminar assessment efforts, as broadly illustrated in Table 27 (p. 59). While these measures are not cited as frequently as findings on other first-year seminar objectives and outcomes, they provide a reminder of the wide range of assessment findings that provide metrics of effectiveness and help improve the course as well as suggest emergent outcomes of interest for first-year seminars.

Conclusion

While assessment is a critical component of course success and long-term sustainability for first-year seminars as a campus initiative, it appears to be an area of the course that is in great need of improvement. For example, barely half of 2009 National Survey respondents participated in assessment or evaluation activities for their first-year seminars since fall 2006. This lack of assessment activities and results negatively impacts the ability of first-year seminar faculty, staff, and leadership to maintain the relevance and excellence of the course and puts it in a vulnerable position with respect to addressing institutional calls for accountability. Further, there appears to be a disconnect between the objectives identified for first-year seminars and the outcomes that are used to measure the course. It is likely that this disconnect is at least in part due to an overreliance upon easily measured but incomplete metrics of success, such as retention, satisfaction, and grade point average, rather than more direct measures of performance and seminar outcomes.

On the other hand, these national data provide several indices of success with respect to first-year seminar assessment, particularly regarding to the diversity of approaches. For example, while quantitative methodologies still dominate the assessment landscape, 2009 National Survey data show that qualitative methodologies are also used to evaluate these courses at many colleges and universities across the country. Further, there is a blend of institutionally developed survey tools and off-the-shelf instruments as well as a range of national surveys used to collect feedback about first-year seminars. Additionally, open-ended feedback on significant first-year seminar assessment findings yielded positive results on a number of outcome measures and success metrics, most notably retention, student satisfaction with the course, academic performance and development, and student/faculty interaction. Finally, several new categories of open-ended responses indicated that first-year seminar results are being used to enhance the delivery and impact of the seminar and chart the pursuit of course learning objectives.

Implications for Practice

The findings presented throughout this research report briefly illustrate the trends and themes that have emerged by examining current national data on first-year seminars. Though the descriptive statistics allow the seminars to be categorized and compared across various institutional characteristics for a broad conceptualization, it is abundantly clear that each seminar is still uniquely defined and administered in accordance with the institution's goals and mission. Conclusions and implications were provided throughout each section following the presentation of the data. Nonetheless, a number of practical implications for administrators and practitioners remain.

Possible Effects From Budget Cuts

As colleges and universities continue to absorb the financial burden of decreased state appropriations and institution-wide budget cuts, seminar administrators likely felt the seismic repercussions of reduced financial support. Well over half (57.2%) of the survey respondents for 2009 National Survey reported that the approximate class size for a seminar section was more than 20 students. This was substantially higher compared to the 2006 National Survey results[7] that found 44.2% of survey respondents reported that a class size for a seminar section was more than 20 students, a 13.0 percentage point difference in only three years.

Yet, number of seminar sections, length of seminar, and seminar instructor—all seminar components subjected to budget cuts—remained unchanged since 2006. Though it is difficult to interpret the evidence presented with regards to the effects of available funding on first-year seminars, anecdotal evidence suggest that seminar administrators are increasingly subjected to budget deficits. Campus administrators, faculty, and staff must prepare for the decrease in not only financial stability, but also resource and staff availability. Further, the evidence presented throughout this research brief suggests that seminars serve as a vital transitional program for first-year students, supporting other national research (Brownell & Swaner, 2010; Leskes & Miller, 2006; Pascarella & Terenzini, 2005). In the face of massive cuts at the programmatic and personnel level, first-year seminars must continue to provide concrete and substantive evidence on the impact of the seminar on a number of institution- and student-level outcomes.

Simultaneously, the evidence presented within the assessment section indicates that institutions are not collecting assessment data in a manner that appropriately supports the effectiveness of their seminar objectives. Only half of the respondents (56.5%) definitively indicated formally

---

[7] The response sets for the survey question asking respondents to *Approximate class size for each first-year seminar section* differed slightly between the 2006 and 2009 Survey. However, using 20 students as a cut-off provides a conservative comparison in the trend of class size over the two survey cycles. Further, this cut-off has become an industry standard, due to the prominence of its use by *US News & World Report*.

assessing or evaluating the seminar since 2006. This lack of assessment and, perhaps, overreliance on nonspecific institutional data collected from national surveys and easily obtainable institution-level student success indicators (i.e., grade point average, grades, retention, and the like) restricts seminar administrators' ability to quantify student success and justify proper funding.

The Disconnect

First-year seminars are considered the connective thread for first-year experiences (e.g., providing additional orientation to campus resources, creating a sense of belonging, providing additional information about proper study skills). However the content and format of the seminar may be defined, the seminar is framed around predetermined course objectives and topics that align with its purpose and goals. Yet, results from the 2009 National Survey suggest that a disconnect exists between course objectives, course topics, and assessment outcomes. As illustrated earlier in this research brief, the three most important course objectives were (a) *develop academic skills* (54.6%), (b) *develop connection with the institution* (50.2%), and (c) *provide orientation to various campus resources and services* (47.6%); while the three most highly reported seminar topics were (a) *campus resources* (42.4%), (b) *study skills* (39.8%), and (c) *academic planning/advising* (35.7%). The predetermined course objectives appear to strike a balance between academic preparation and integration/sense of belonging; whereas, the three course topics survey respondents identified as the most important were primarily academic. Perhaps a clear, though minor misalignment between the seminar's objective and the academic topics within the seminar exists.

However, an even greater disconnect—outlined here and in the assessment section—exists between course objectives and formal assessment and evaluation of the seminar. As presented earlier, the three most important assessment outcomes were (a) *persistence to sophomore year*, (b) *satisfaction with faculty*, and (c) *satisfaction with the institution*. Though persistence is often an obtainable institutional-level data point and satisfaction with faculty and the institution is measured via course evaluations, these assessment outcomes do not align with the course objectives most often reported. Given the increasing pressure from internal and external constituents on the accountability of higher education, it becomes imperative for seminars to accurately and consistently measure course objectives set forth by seminar administrators and students' success and/or development across these objectives. In other words, seminars must begin to rely more heavily on assessing and evaluating practices.

Pedagogical Potential

About half of the institutions that have a first-year seminar incorporate an online component, and only half of the respondents indicate that students are required to participate in an online component. Further, the reported low numbers of online-only sections within the 2009 data (14.5%) suggest that first-year seminars continue to rely on the dominant pedagogical structure of face-to-face instruction despite technological advances within the classroom, including online instruction. Evidence from the open-ended survey item asking respondents to describe the online components that are included in the course suggest that technology is primarily used as a convenience (e.g., repository for course documents, portal for submitting assignments, online tutorial) rather than a resource for active learning. Further, today's first-year students were born in a readily accessible online age, where social media dominates their everyday interactions. Yet, seminars—and arguably all other college courses—have not welcomed the use of social media within the classroom. Incorporating active-learning exercises that utilize online components would likely placate student demand for use of technology while simultaneously instructing them on proper online academic use. The use of digital resources, such as Skype, iChat, iMovie, and Prezi, should not just be encouraged as an innovative mechanism for course assignments, but also for content delivery.

Similar to online components, survey respondents reported that only 40.3% of seminars incorporate a service-learning component into the seminar, and 35.7% of seminar sections were linked to other courses. These low aggregate findings suggest that service-learning and linked courses (i.e., learning communities) are not being connected to the seminar to their fullest pedagogical potential. Further, responses to open-ended questions indicate that in many instances these course practices are not being used in a very innovative fashion and have significantly unrealized pedagogical potential. The Association of American Colleges and Universities (AAC&U) identified these two components as powerful curricular and pedagogic practices that help advance students' development across a number of learning outcomes (Leskes & Miller, 2006). Using service-learning activities and purposeful linked courses within the seminar in a constructive and meaningful way provides an additional beyond-the-classroom connection for first-year students.

This is not to dismiss the valuable resources often provided and obtained through the first-year seminar. A recent study using a large, national pretest-posttest longitudinal dataset examined the effects of the first-year seminar on the need to engage in cognitive activities and found that participation in first-year seminars significantly increases (a) students' need for cognition; (b) the likelihood of students integrating ideas, information, and experiences from class into the real world; and (c) academic challenge and effort in class (Padgett & Keup, 2010). The researchers posit,

> [T]hese findings legitimize first-year seminars as a vehicle for enhancing students' integration of ideas, information, and experiences....suggests that first-year seminars are academically challenging and require a higher level of effort than some perceived. Further, these research findings can help refine learning outcomes and program goals for first-year seminars at the institutional level as well as encourage faculty and staff who oversee and teach in these programs to capitalize on course pedagogies, administration, and structures that facilitate academic integration and challenge in service of cognitive development among students. (p. 18)

The findings from Padgett and Keup (2010) imply that simple participation in a first-year seminar does not necessarily guarantee successful transitions or growth across measurable learning outcomes. Rather, it is the pedagogical practices and incorporation of vetted good practices within the seminar that facilitate student development. In accordance with results from the 2009 National Survey, findings from Padgett and Keup suggest that a more integrative and challenging approach can simultaneously foster orientation and students' demand for academic rigor.

Assessment

Approximately one third of the institutions reported that no formal assessment process was conducted within the past three years. The open-ended responses within the 2009 Survey suggest colleges and universities that did not formally assess their seminar have a desire for formal assessment. Of the institutions that conducted a formal assessment of the seminar, 94.9% relied heavily on student course evaluations. In addition, 75.3% of institutions that formally assessed the seminar analyzed institutional data (e.g., grade point average, retention rates, graduation rates), 84.0% used a locally developed survey, and 52.4% used a national survey instrument. Of the respondents who assessed the seminar using a national survey instrument, 73.8% used the National Survey of Student Engagement and 35.3% used the Freshman Survey sponsored by the Cooperative Institutional Research Program—an instrument designed to identify input variables rather than measure outcome measure. It is encouraging that seminar administrators are employing a number of assessment tools and techniques to gauge the effectiveness of seminar participation. However, caution should be taken when using large, national surveys, particularly as a primary assessment tool of the seminar. These national surveys—while invaluable assessment and benchmarking tools that measure student experiences and engagement—tend to have few questions related to the first-year seminar experience. Institutions must employ targeted assessments of the first-year seminar to have a comprehensive understanding of the effectiveness of their practices and pedagogical techniques, which may explain the larger proportion of respondents who use locally developed instruments, as reported in the Survey. National surveys, then, are best served as a companion tool when examining specific program-level initiatives, such as first-year seminars.

Similarly, additional caution should be taken when assessing student growth or development across predetermined learning outcomes within the seminar. An often unidentified mistake when assessing the success of a learning outcome is not accounting for selection bias within the student sample. In other words, one cannot definitively claim that the first-year seminar significantly contributes to gains across a learning outcome. This is because first-year students are likely not randomly assigned to participate in the seminar; they self-select to enroll (if the seminar is not required for all students). For a complete and comprehensive comparison, an assessment of the learning outcome for students who do not participate in the seminar would need to be conducted simultaneously. Only then can institutional personnel definitively state that the first-year seminar significantly impacted first-year students' development on any learning outcome.

Conclusion

Within the aggregate, the 2009 Survey provides the most recent national snapshot of first-year seminars. As the results were disaggregated and compared across institutional controls, institutional patterns emerged. These comparative data allow institutions to reassess and evaluate their current understanding of how the first-year seminar is defined and used at the national level. In the end, national data should inform and guide. Each institution uniquely defines and administers its first-year seminar based on the purpose it serves within the context of the goals and mission of the institution. In other words, there is no perfect model for the first-year seminar. National data can have profound implications for practice, but the success of the seminar relies entirely on how institutions incorporate this information to best serve their first-year students.

Appendix A: Survey Methodology

Population

The access population for the 2009 National Survey of First-Year Seminars were chief academic officers, chief executive officers, and/or chief student affairs officers at regionally accredited, not-for-profit, undergraduate-serving institutions of higher education. This population was drawn from the electronic edition of the *2010 Higher Education Directory*. Though the chief academic officers, chief executive officers, and/or chief student affairs officers are likely well informed about their institution's first-year seminar, these contacts were instructed to forward the e-mail *if it would be more appropriate for another person on your campus to complete this survey*. As such, our population of interest were the individuals who were the most knowledgeable about the first-year seminar at each institution.

Survey Administration

The survey content was created and constructed by the National Resource Center for The First-Year Experience and Students in Transition (NRC). The dissemination and administration of the survey instrument was conducted by StudentVoice, an online assessment program that, among other specialized assessment platforms, collects data using web-based technology. StudentVoice oversaw the survey administration and general data management, as well as housed the survey link.

On October 30, 2009, an invitation to participate in the Survey was sent to the chief academic officer—or the chief executive officer if there was no listing for the chief academic officer in the *2010 Higher Education Directory*. If neither the chief academic officer nor the chief executive officer were listed within the *Higher Education Directory*, the institution was omitted from the study. Further, nonverified or undeliverable e-mail accounts were also omitted from the study. The invitation served three primary purposes: (a) notifying participants that the NRC was conducting the eighth administration of the Survey; (b) providing detailed information about when they could anticipate receiving a link to the survey instrument; and (c) confirming that the participant was the appropriate contact or representative who could accurately provide information about the first-year seminar, and if not, request the correct campus contact information.

The Survey was launched on November 4, 2009, and a total of 2,519 verified participants were e-mailed the survey link and the deadline to participate (December 11, 2009). Following the launch date, four follow-up reminders were sent to nonrespondents. The first reminder e-mail was sent on November 10 to the chief academic officer; the second reminder e-mail was sent on November 17 to the chief executive officer, with a subsequent reminder e-mail sent on November 23; the third reminder e-mail was sent December 1 to the chief student affairs officer; the final reminder was sent December 8 to all three institutional contacts (i.e., chief academic officer, chief executive officer, and the chief student affairs officer). The survey administration ended on December 11, 2009 at 5:00 p.m., and the survey link was officially disabled on December 15, 2009.

Incentives were provided to promote and encourage survey responses. Survey participants were informed in the invitation to participate and follow-up letters that completion of the Survey would enter their institution into a random drawing for one of three registration waivers to the 29th Annual Conference on The First-Year Experience or one of 10 institutional subscriptions to *E-Source for College Transitions*, an online professional newsletter published by NRC. Further, survey respondents were informed that their survey responses would remain confidential unless they self-selected to publicly share their responses through a confirmation question that concluded the Survey.

A total of 1,019 institutions participated in the 2009 survey administration, indicating a 40.5% response rate—a reasonable response rate for a web-based survey. The response rate is a slight increase from the 2006 administration (36.6%) and a significant increase to the 2003 administration (23.7%). Of the 1,019 total respondents, 890 institutions (87.3%) indicated their institution offered a first-year seminar, while 129 institutions (12.7%) indicated they did not offer a seminar or did not know if they offered a seminar.

Analyses

The original measure for first-year class size had a response set of 10 continuous iterations of class size (ranging from *less than 500, 501–1,000*, and increasing in intervals of 1,000 up to *more than 5,000*). First-year class size was recoded into a six interval response set because of the low number of institutions in some of the higher response sets. Collapsing some of the response sets with lower responses increases the statistical power of each response set for comparative analyses. Furthermore, *other* was a viable response option for respondents selecting a discrete type of first-year seminar on their campus. Only 22 respondents identified their seminar as *other*. Given the low frequency and weak statistical power of this category and the ambiguity of *other* as a seminar option, *other* was dropped from comparative analyses involving seminar type.

The analyses of the sample data were primarily conducted at the descriptive level. Appendix D provides a comprehensive frequency distribution and sample percentages for each item. Further, the frequencies were tabulated for the sample in the aggregate (total) and across institutional type, control, size, and seminar type. To test for significance across group type, chi-square analyses were conducted across institution type (two-year, four-year), control (public, private), first-year class size (less than 500, 501-1,000, 1,001-2,000, 2,001-3,000, 3,001-4,000, and 4,001+), and seminar type (extended orientation, academic with uniform content, academic on various topics, preprofessional or discipline-linked, basic study skills, and hybrid). Note that significant effects are not represented within Appendix D but are reported throughout the research brief.

Appendix B: Survey Instrument

2009 National Survey on First-Year Seminars

This survey is dedicated to gathering information regarding first-year seminars. The survey should take 30-45 minutes to complete. You may exit the survey at any time and return, and your responses will be saved. If you would like a copy of your responses, you will need to print each page of your survey before exiting.

Your responses are important to us, so please respond by December 11, 2009. Thank you.

1 ▪ Full name of institution: _____

2 ▪ City: _____

3 ▪ State: _____

4 ▪ Your name: _____

5 ▪ Title: _____

6 ▪ Mark the appropriate category for your institution:
○ Two-year institution
○ Four-year institution

7 ▪ Mark the appropriate category for your institution:
○ Public
○ Private, not-for-profit
○ Private, for-profit

8 ▪ What is the approximate number of entering first-year students in academic year 2009-2010 at your institution?
○ Less than 500
○ 501 - 1,000
○ 1,001 - 1,500
○ 1,501 - 2,000
○ 2,001 - 2,500
○ 2,501 - 3,000

○ 3,001 - 3,500

○ 3,501 - 4,000

○ 4,001 - 5,000

○ More than 5,000

9 ▪ First-year seminars are courses designed to enhance the academic skills and/or social development of first-year college students.

Does your institution, including any department or division, offer one or more first-year seminar-type courses?

○ I don't know *(Go to end)*

○ No *(Go to end)*

○ Yes *(Go to Question 10)*

10 ▪ What is the approximate percentage of first-year students who take a first-year seminar course on your campus?

○ Less than 10%

○ 20% - 29%

○ 30% - 39%

○ 40% - 49%

○ 50% - 59%

○ 60% - 69%

○ 70% - 79%

○ 80% - 89%

○ 90% - 99%

○ 100%

11 ▪ Approximately how many years has a first-year seminar been offered on your campus?

○ Two years or less

○ Three to 10 years

○ More than 10 years

Types of Seminars Offered

12 ▪ Select each discrete type of first-year seminar that best describes the seminars that exist on your campus: (Check all that apply)

○ **Extended orientation seminar**– Sometimes called freshman orientation, college survival, college transition, or student success course. Content often includes introduction to campus resources, time management, academic and career planning, learning strategies, and an introduction to student development issues.

○ **Academic seminar with generally uniform academic content across sections**– May be an interdisciplinary or theme-oriented course, sometimes part of a general education requirement. Primary focus is on academic theme/discipline, but will often include academic skills components such as critical thinking and expository writing.

○ **Academic seminar on various topics**– Similar to previously mentioned academic seminar except that specific topics vary from section to section.

○ **Preprofessional or discipline-linked seminar**– Designed to prepare students for the demands of the major/discipline and the profession. Generally taught within professional schools or specific disciplines such as engineering, health sciences, business, or education.

○ **Basic study skills seminar**– Offered for academically underprepared students. The focus is on basic academic skills such as grammar, note taking, and reading texts, etc.

○ **Hybrid**– Has elements from two or more types of seminar. *(Go to Question 13)*

○ **Other** *(Go to Question 14)*

13 ■ Please describe the *Hybrid* first-year seminar: _____

_____

14 ■ Please describe the *Other* first-year seminar: _____

_____

Specific Seminar Information

15 ■ If you offer more than one first-year seminar type, select the type with the *highest* total student enrollment:

○ Extended orientation seminar

○ Academic seminar with generally uniform content

○ Academic seminar on various topics

○ Preprofessional or discipline-linked seminar

○ Basic study skills seminar

○ Hybrid

○ Other

Please answer the remaining questions for only the first-year seminar type with the highest total enrollment on your campus.

16 ■ Please indicate the approximate number of sections of this seminar type that will be offered in the 2009-2010 academic year:

○ 0

○ 1 – 10

○ 11 – 20

○ 21 – 30

○ 31 – 40

○ 41 – 50

○ 51 – 60

○ 61 – 70

○ 71 – 80

○ 81 – 90

○ 91 – 100

○ Over 100

The Students

17 ▪ What is the approximate class size for each first-year seminar section?

○ 10 students or fewer

○ 11 – 15

○ 16 – 19

○ 20 – 24

○ 25 – 29

○ 30 or more

18 ▪ What is the approximate percentage of first-year students *required* to take the first-year seminar?

○ None are required to take it

○ Less than 10%

○ 10% - 19%

○ 20% - 29%

○ 30% - 39%

○ 40% - 49%

○ 50% - 59%

○ 60% - 69%

○ 70% - 79%

○ 80% - 89%

○ 90% - 99%

○ 100%

19 ▪ Which students, by category, are *required* to take the first-year seminar? (Check all that apply.)

○ None are required to take it

○ All first-year students are required to take it

○ Academically underprepared students

○ First-generation students

○ Honors students

○ International students

○ Learning community participants

○ Preprofessional students (e.g., prelaw, premed)

○ Provisionally admitted students

○ Student-athletes
○ Students participating in dual-enrollment programs
○ Students residing within a particular residence hall
○ Students within specific majors (please list) _____
○ Transfer students
○ TRIO participants
○ Undeclared students
○ Other (please specify) _____

20 ▪ Please identify unique subpopulations of students for which *special sections* of the first-year seminar are offered: (Check all that apply)
○ No special sections are offered
○ Academically underprepared students
○ First-generation students
○ Honors students
○ International students
○ Learning community participants
○ Preprofessional students (e.g., prelaw, premed)
○ Provisionally admitted students
○ Student-athletes
○ Students participating in dual-enrollment programs
○ Students residing within a particular residence hall
○ Students within specific majors (please list) _____
○ Transfer students
○ TRIO participants
○ Undeclared students
○ Other (please specify) _____

The Instructors

21 ▪ Who teaches the first-year seminar? (Check all that apply)
○ Adjunct faculty *(Go to Question 30, Question 35)*
○ Full-time non-tenure-track faculty
○ Graduate students *(Go to Question 28, Question 34)*
○ Student affairs professionals *(Go to Question 29, Question 32)*
○ Tenure-track faculty *(Go to Question 27, Question 31)*
○ Undergraduate students *(Go to Question 22)*
○ Other campus professionals (please specify) *(Go to Question 33)* _____

22 ▪ If undergraduate students assist in the first-year seminar, what is their role? (Check all that apply)

○ They teach independently.

○ They teach as a part of a team.

○ They assist the instructor, but do not teach.

○ Other (please specify) _____

23 ▪ Indicate the approximate percentage of sections that are team taught:

○ No sections are team taught.

○ Less than 10%

○ 10% - 19%

○ 20% - 29%

○ 30% - 39%

○ 40% - 49%

○ 50% - 59%

○ 60% - 69%

○ 70% - 79%

○ 80% - 89%

○ 90% - 99%

○ 100%

24 ▪ Please describe the team configurations (e.g., two faculty, one faculty and one advisor) if they are used in your first-year seminar courses: _____

_____

25 ▪ Are any first-year students intentionally placed in first-year seminar sections taught by their academic advisors?

○ I don't know

○ No

○ Yes (Go to Question 26)

26 ▪ What is the approximate percentage of students placed in sections with their academic advisors?

○ Less than 10%

○ 10% - 19%

○ 20% - 29%

○ 30% - 39%

○ 40% - 49%

○ 50% - 59%

○ 60% - 69%
○ 70% - 79%
○ 80% - 89%
○ 90% - 99%
○ 100%

27 ▪ Faculty who teach the first-year seminar teach the course as: (Check all that apply)
○ An overload course
○ Part of regular teaching load
○ Other (please specify) _____

28 ▪ Graduate students who teach the first-year seminar teach the course as: (Check all that apply)
○ An assigned responsibility
○ An extra responsibility
○ Other (please specify) _____

29 ▪ Student affairs professionals who teach the first-year seminar teach the course as: (Check all that apply)
○ An assigned responsibility
○ An extra responsibility
○ Other (please specify) _____

30 ▪ What type of compensation is offered to adjunct faculty for teaching the first-year seminar? (Check all that apply)
○ No compensation is offered
○ Graduate student support *(Go to Question 41)*
○ Release time *(Go to Question 40)*
○ Stipend *(Go to Question 35)*
○ Unrestricted professional development funds *(Go to Question 42)*
○ Other (please specify) _____

31 ▪ What type of compensation is offered to tenure-track faculty for teaching the first-year seminar? (Check all that apply)
○ No compensation is offered
○ Graduate student support
○ Release time
○ Stipend *(Go to Question 36)*
○ Unrestricted professional development funds
○ Other (please specify) _____

32 ▪ What type of compensation is offered to student affairs professionals for teaching the first-year seminar? (Check all that apply)

○ No compensation is offered

○ Graduate student support

○ Release time

○ Stipend *(Go to Question 37)*

○ Unrestricted professional development funds

○ Other (please specify) _____

33 ▪ What type of compensation is offered to other campus professionals for teaching the first-year seminar? (Check all that apply)

○ No compensation is offered

○ Graduate student support

○ Release time

○ Stipend *(Go to Question 38)*

○ Unrestricted professional development funds

○ Other (please specify) _____

34 ▪ What type of compensation is offered to graduate students for teaching the first-year seminar? (Check all that apply)

○ No compensation is offered

○ Stipend *(Go to Question 39)*

○ Other (please specify) _____

35 ▪ Please indicate the total amount of the stipend per class for adjunct faculty:

○ 500 or less

○ $501 - $1,000

○ $2,001 - $2,500

○ $2,501 - $3,000

○ $3,001 - $3,500

○ $4,001 - $4,500

○ $4,501 - $5,000

○ More than $5,000

36 ▪ Please indicate the total amount of the stipend per class for tenure-track faculty:

○ 500 or less

○ $501 - $1,000

○ $2,001 - $2,500

○ $2,501 - $3,000

○ $3,001 - $3,500

○ $4,001 - $4,500
○ $4501 - $5000
○ More than $5000

37 ▪ Please indicate the total amount of the stipend per class for student affairs professionals:
○ 500 or less
○ $501 - $1,000
○ $2,001 - $2,500
○ $2,501 - $3,000
○ $3,001 - $3,500
○ $4,001 - $4,500
○ $4,501 - $5,000
○ More than $5,000

38 ▪ Please indicate the total amount of the stipend per class for other campus professionals:
○ 500 or less
○ $501 - $1,000
○ $2,001 - $2,500
○ $2,501 - $3,000
○ $3,001 - $3,500
○ $4,001 - $4,500
○ $4,501 - $5,000
○ More than $5,000

39 ▪ Please indicate the total amount of the stipend per class for graduate students:
○ 500 or less
○ $501 - $1,000
○ $2,001 - $2,500
○ $2,501 - $3,000
○ $3,001 - $3,500
○ $4,001 - $4,500
○ $4,501 - $5,000
○ More than $5,000

40 ▪ Please indicate the amount of release time: _____

41 ▪ Please indicate the number of hours per week of graduate student support: _____

42 ▪ Please describe the unrestricted professional development funds:_____

_____

43 ▪ Is instructor training *offered* for first-year seminar instructors?

○ I don't know

○ No

○ Yes *(Go to Question 45)*

44 ▪ Is instructor training *required* for first-year seminar instructors?

○ I don't know

○ No

○ Yes

45 ▪ How long is new instructor training?

○ Half a day or less

○ 1 day

○ 2 days

○ 3 days

○ 4 days

○ 1 week

○ Other (please specify) _____

The Course

46 ▪ What is the typical length of a section of the first-year seminar?

○ Half a semester

○ One quarter

○ One semester

○ One year

○ Other (please specify) _____

47 ▪ How is the first-year seminar graded?

○ Pass/fail

○ Letter grade

○ No grade

○ Other (please specify) _____

48 ▪ Does the first-year seminar carry academic credit?

○ I don't know

○ No

○ Yes (Go to *Question 49, Question 50*)

49 ▪ How many credits does the first-year seminar carry?

○ 1
○ 2
○ 3
○ 4
○ 5
○ More than 5

50 ▪ How is the first-year seminar credit applied? (Check all that apply)

○ As an elective
○ Toward general education requirements
○ Toward major requirements
○ Other (please specify) _____

51 ▪ How many total classroom contact hours are there per week in the first-year seminar?

○ 1
○ 2
○ 3
○ 4
○ 5
○ More than 5

52 ▪ Do any sections include a service-learning component (i.e., nonremunerative service as part of a course)?

○ I don't know
○ No
○ Yes *(Go to Question 53)*

53 ▪ Please describe the service-learning component of the seminar: _____

_____

_____

54 ▪ Are any sections linked to one or more other courses (i.e., learning community —enrolling a cohort of students into two or more courses)?

○ I don't know
○ No
○ Yes *(Go to Question 56)*

55 ▪ Do any sections incorporate a first-year/summer reading program component?

○ I don't know

○ No

○ Yes

56 ▪ Please describe the learning community: _____

_____

_____

57 ▪ Do any sections incorporate online components?

○ I don't know

○ No

○ Yes *(Go to Question 58, Question 59)*

58 ▪ Please describe the online components that are included in the course: _____

_____

59 ▪ Are there any online-only sections?

○ I don't know

○ No

○ Yes *(Go to Question 60)*

60 ▪ Please indicate the approximate percentage of online-only sections:

○ Less than 10%

○ 10% - 19%

○ 20% - 29%

○ 30% - 39%

○ 40% - 49%

○ 50% - 59%

○ 60% - 69%

○ 70% - 79%

○ 80% - 89%

○ 90% - 99%

○ 100%

The Administration

61 ▪ What campus unit directly administers the first-year seminar?

○ Academic affairs

○ Academic department(s) (please list) _____

○ College or school (e.g., College of Liberal Arts)

○ First-year program office

○ Student affairs

○ Other (please specify) _____

62 ▪ Is there a dean/director/coordinator of the first-year seminar?

○ I don't know

○ No

○ Yes *(Go to Question 63)*

63 ▪ Does the dean/director/coordinator of the first-year seminar work full time or less than full time in this position?

○ Full time (approximately 40 hours per week)

○ Less than full time *(Go to Question 64)*

64 ▪ Does the dean/director/coordinator have another position on campus?

○ I don't know

○ No

○ Yes *(Go to Question 65)*

65 ▪ The dean/director/coordinator's other campus role is as a/an: (Check all that apply)

○ Academic affairs administrator

○ Faculty member

○ Student affairs administrator

○ Other (please specify) _____

Assessment and Evaluation

66 ▪ Select the *three* most important *course objectives* for the first-year seminar:

○ Create common first-year experience

○ Develop a connection with the institution

○ Develop academic skills

○ Develop financial literacy

○ Develop support network/friendships

○ Develop writing skills

○ Improve sophomore return rates

○ Increase student/faculty interaction

○ Introduce a discipline

○ Provide orientation to campus resources and services

○ Self-exploration/personal development

○ Encourage arts participation

○ Other (please specify) _____

67 ▪ Select the *three* most important *topics* that compose the content of this first-year seminar:
○ Academic planning/advising
○ Career exploration/preparation
○ Campus resources
○ College policies and procedures
○ Critical thinking
○ Diversity issues
○ Financial literacy
○ Health and wellness
○ Relationship issues (e.g., interpersonal skills, conflict resolution)
○ Specific disciplinary topic
○ Study skills
○ Time management
○ Writing skills (Go to *Question 68*)
○ Other (please specify) _____

68 ▪ Briefly describe up to *three* assignments or activities used to promote the development of

writing skills in the seminar: _____

_____

_____

69 ▪ Please list up to *three* elements or aspects of your first-year seminar that you consider inno-

vative or especially successful: _____

_____

_____

70 ▪ Has your first-year seminar been formally assessed or evaluated since fall 2006?
○ I don't know *(Go to Question 83)*
○ No *(Go to Question 83)*
○ Yes *(Go to Question 71)*

What type of assessment was conducted?
71 ▪ Analysis of institutional data (e.g., GPA, retention rates, graduation)
○ I don't know
○ No
○ Yes

72 ▪ Focus groups with instructors
○ I don't know
○ No
○ Yes

73 ▪ Focus groups with students
○ I don't know
○ No
○ Yes

74 ▪ Individual interviews with instructors
○ I don't know
○ No
○ Yes

75 ▪ Individual interviews with students
○ I don't know
○ No
○ Yes

76 ▪ Student course evaluation
○ I don't know
○ No
○ Yes

77 ▪ Survey instrument
○ I don't know
○ No
○ Yes *(Go to Question 78)*

78 ▪ What type of survey instrument did your institution use to assess or evaluate the first-year seminar? (Check all that apply)
○ I don't know
○ A locally developed (i.e., home-grown) survey
○ A national survey (e.g., NSSE, CCSSE, CIRP, EBI) *(Go to Question 79)*

79 ▪ If you used a national survey, please identify the survey/s: (Check all that apply)
○ Community College Survey of Student Engagement (CCSSE)
○ Cooperative Institutional Research Program (CIRP) Freshman Survey
○ Cooperative Institutional Research Program (CIRP) Your First College Year (YFCY)
○ First-Year Initiative (FYI)
○ National Survey of Student Engagement (NSSE)
○ Other (please specify) _____

80 ▪ Please describe any other types of assessment or evaluation that were conducted: _____

_____

_____

81 ▪ Select each outcome that was measured: (Check all that apply)
○ Connections with peers
○ Grade point average
○ Out-of-class student/faculty interaction
○ Participation in campus activities
○ Persistence to graduation
○ Persistence to sophomore year
○ Satisfaction with faculty
○ Satisfaction with the institution
○ Use of campus services
○ Other (please specify) _____

82 ▪ Please describe the most significant findings from your assessment and evaluation of first-

year seminar outcomes: _____

_____

_____

83 ▪ It is our practice to make available specific and general information gathered from this survey. In general, findings from the survey are reported in aggregate, but we may identify individual institutions that have agreed to allow their responses to be shared on request. Please select the appropriate response:

○ You may share my survey responses.
○ Please do not share my survey responses.

Appendix C: Respondents to the 2009 National Survey of First-Year Seminar[8]

Institution	City	State
Abraham Baldwin Agricultural College	Tifton	Georgia
Albany State University	Albany	Georgia
Albertus Magnus College	New Haven	Connecticut
Albion College	Albion	Michigan
Albright College	Reading	Pennsylvania
Allen Community College	Iola	Kansas
Alvernia University	Reading	Pennsylvania
Alverno College	Milwaukee	Wisconsin
Amarillo College	Amarillo	Texas
American International College	Springfield	Massachusetts
Angelo State University	San Angelo	Texas
Arkansas Northeastern College	Blytheville	Arkansas
Arkansas State University	Jonesboro	Arkansas
Arkansas State University Beebe	Beebe	Arkansas
Arkansas State University - Newport	Newport	Arkansas
Art Institutes International Minnesota	Minneapolis	Minnesota
Asheville-Buncombe Technical Community College	Asheville	North Carolina
Auburn University at Montgomery	Montgomery	Alabama
Augsburg College	Minneapolis	Minnesota
Augusta State University	Augusta	Georgia
Austin College	Sherman	Texas
Averett University	Danville	Virginia
Avila University	Kansas City	Missouri
Babson College	Babson Park	Massachusetts

[8] This is a partial list ($n = 493$) of total respondents ($n = 1,019$). Institutions were provided the opportunity to opt-out of being publicly identified as a survey respondent.

Baldwin Wallace College	Berea	Ohio
Bard College	Annandale on Hudson	New York
Bard College at Simon's Rock	Great Barrington	Massachusetts
Bay de Noc Community College	Escanaba	Michigan
Baylor University	Waco	Texas
Beacon College	Leesburg	Florida
Bellingham Technical College	Bellingham	Washington
Benedictine College	Atchison	Kansas
Benjamin Franklin Institute of Technology	Boston	Massachusetts
Bennett College for Women	Greensboro	North Carolina
Bentley University	Waltham	Massachusetts
Berry College	Mount Berry	Georgia
Bethany College	Bethany	West Virginia
Bethel College	North Newton	Kansas
Bethel University	McKenzie	Tennessee
Bethel University	St. Paul	Minnesota
Big Sandy Community and Technical College	Prestonsburg	Kentucky
Binghamton University	Binghamton	New York
Blinn College	Brenham	Texas
Blue Mountain Community College	Pendleton	Oregon
Bluefield College	Bluefield	Virginia
Bluffton University	Bluffton	Ohio
Brescia University	Owensboro	Kentucky
Brevard College	Brevard	North Carolina
Brewton-Parker College	Mount Vernon	Georgia
Bridgemont Community & Technical College	Montgomery	West Virginia
Bridgewater State College	Bridgewater	Massachusetts
Brigham Young University	Provo	Utah
Brown Mackie College	Indianapolis	Indiana
Brown Mackie College	Akron	Ohio
Brown University	Providence	Rhode Island
Bryant & Stratton College	Albany	New York
Bryant & Stratton College	Virginia Beach	Virginia
Bucknell University	Lewisburg	Pennsylvania
Caldwell College	Caldwell	New Jersey
California State University, Chico	Chico	California
California State University, Dominguez Hills	Carson	California
California State University, Northridge	Northridge	California
Cameron University	Lawton	Oklahoma

Cankdeska Cikana Community College	Fort Totten	North Dakota
Cape Cod Community College	West Barnstable	Massachusetts
Capital University	Columbus	Ohio
Cardinal Stritch University	Milwaukee	Wisconsin
Carleton College	Northfield	Minnesota
Carson-Newman College	Jefferson City	Tennessee
Central Georgia Technical College	Macon	Georgia
Central Lakes College	Brainerd	Minnesota
Central Maine Community College	Auburn	Maine
Central Michigan University	Mount Pleasant	Michigan
Central Wyoming College	Riverton	Wyoming
Century College	White Bear Lake	Minnesota
Charleston Southern University	Charleston	South Carolina
Chicago State University	Chicago	Illinois
Chipola College	Marianna	Florida
Claremont McKenna College	Claremont	California
Clark State Community College	Springfield	Ohio
Clarke College	Dubuque	Iowa
Cleveland Institute of Music	Cleveland	Ohio
Cleveland State University	Cleveland	Ohio
Clinton Community College	Plattsburgh	New York
Coastal Carolina University	Conway	South Carolina
Coe College	Cedar Rapids	Iowa
College for Creative Studies	Detroit	Michigan
College of Alameda	Alameda	California
College of Eastern Utah	Price	Utah
College of Mount Saint Vincent	Riverdale	New York
College of Saint Benedict/Saint John's University	Collegeville	Minnesota
College of Southern Maryland	LaPlata	Maryland
College of the Sequoias	Visalia	California
CollegeAmerica	Ft. Collins	Colorado
Colorado State University - Pueblo	Pueblo	Colorado
Columbia Basin College	Pasco	Washington
Columbia College	Columbia	South Carolina
Columbia College Chicago	Chicago	Illinois
Concordia University	St. Paul	Minnesota
Concordia University Wisconsin	Mequon	Wisconsin
Corban College and Graduate School	Salem	Oregon
Cornerstone University	Grand Rapids	Michigan
Corning Community College	Corning	New York

Creighton University	Omaha	Nebraska
Cumberland County College	Vineland	New Jersey
Curry College	Milton	Massachusetts
Cuyamaca College	El Cajon	California
Darton College	Albany	Georgia
Delaware County Community College	Media	Pennsylvania
Dixie State College of Utah	St. George	Utah
East Los Angeles College	Monterey Park	California
Eastern Illinois University	Charleston	Illinois
Eastern Kentucky University	Richmond	Kentucky
Eastern Mennonite University	Harrisonburg	Virginia
Eastern Michigan University	Ypsilanti	Michigan
Eastern New Mexico University	Portales	New Mexico
Eastern University	St. Davids	Pennsylvania
Eastern Wyoming College	Torrington	Wyoming
East-West University	Chicago	Illinois
Ecclesia College	Springdale	Arkansas
Eckerd College	St. Petersburg	Florida
EDP College of Puerto Rico	Hato Rey	Pennsylvania
Elgin Community College	Elgin	Illinois
Elizabeth City State University	Elizabeth City	North Carolina
Elizabethtown College	Elizabethtown	Pennsylvania
Elmhurst College	Elmhurst	Illinois
Emporia State University	Emporia	Kansas
Eureka College	Eureka	Illinois
Everest University	Orlando	Florida
Everett Community College	Everett	Washington
Excelsior College	Albany	New York
Fayetteville State University	Fayetteville	North Carolina
Florida International University	Miami	Florida
Florida Keys Community College	Key West	Florida
Florida National College	Hialeah	Florida
Framingham State College	Framingham	Massachusetts
Franklin College	Franklin	Indiana
Franklin Pierce University	Rindge	New Hampshire
Franklin W. Olin College of Engineering	Needham	Massachusetts
Frederick Community College	Frederick	Maryland
Fulton-Montgomery Community College	Johnstown	New York
Furman University	Greenville	North Carolina
Gainesville State College	Gainesville	Georgia

Garden City Community College	Garden City	Kansas
Gardner-Webb University	Boiling Spring	North Carolina
Geneva College	Beaver Falls	Pennsylvania
George Fox University	Newberg	Oregon
Georgia College & State University	Milledgeville	Georgia
Georgia Institute of Technology	Atlanta	Georgia
Georgia Southern University	Statesboro	Georgia
Grace University	Omaha	Nebraska
Grand Rapids Community College	Grand Rapids	Michigan
Grantham University	Kansas City	Missouri
Grays Harbor College	Aberdeen	Washington
Greenville Technical College	Greenville	South Carolina
Guilford College	Greensboro	North Carolina
Guilford Technical Community College	Jamestown	North Carolina
Hamline University	St. Paul	Minnesota
Hampden-Sydney College	Hampden-Sydney	Virginia
Hanover College	Hanover	Indiana
Hardin-Simmons University	Abilene	Texas
Heidelberg University	Tiffin	Ohio
Henderson State University	Arkadelphia	Arkansas
Herkimer County Community College	Herkimer	New York
Hilbert College	Hamburg	New York
Hill College	Hillsboro	Texas
Hiram College	Hiram	Ohio
Hollins University	Roanoke	Virginia
Hopkinsville Community College	Hopkinsville	Kentucky
Houston Baptist University	Houston	Texas
Howard Community College	Columbia	Maryland
Huntington University	Huntington	Indiana
Husson University	Bangor	Maine
Idaho State University	Pocatello	Idaho
Illinois State University	Normal	Illinois
Imperial Valley Community College	Imperial	California
Indiana University East	Richmond	Indiana
Indiana University Kokomo	Kokomo	Indiana
Indiana University - Purdue University Indianapolis	Indianapolis	Indiana
Indiana University Southeast	New Albany	Indiana
Institute of American Indian Arts	Santa Fe	New Mexico
Jackson Community College	Jackson	Michigan
Jackson State University	Jackson	Mississippi

Jamestown College	Jamestown	North Dakota
Jefferson College	Hillsboro	Missouri
Jefferson Community & Technical College	Louisville	Kentucky
John Brown University	Siloam Springs	Arkansas
Johnson & Wales University	Charlotte	North Carolina
Johnson College	Scranton	Pennsylvania
Judson University	Elgin	Illinois
Kalamazoo College	Kalamazoo	Michigan
Kankakee Community College	Kankakee	Illinois
Kansas State University	Manhattan	Kansas
Kennesaw State University	Kennesaw	Georgia
Kent State University at Tuscarawas	New Philadelphia	Ohio
Kentucky Wesleyan College	Owensboro	Kentucky
Keystone College	La Plume	Pennsylvania
Kilgore College	Kilgore	Texas
Kuyper College	Grand Rapids	Michigan
LaGuardia Community College	New York	New York
Laguna College of Art + Design	Laguna Beach	California
Lake Land College	Mattoon	Illinois
Lake Michigan College	Benton Harbor	Michigan
Le Moyne College	Syracuse	New York
Lesley University	Cambridge	Massachusetts
Lewis & Clark College	Portland	Oregon
Lincoln University	Jefferson City	Missouri
Loras College	Dubuque	Iowa
Loyola University Maryland	Baltimore	Maryland
Loyola University New Orleans	New Orleans	Louisiana
Macalester College	St. Paul	Minnesota
MacMurray College	Jacksonville	Illinois
Madonna University	Livonia	Michigan
Manchester Community College	Manchester	Connecticut
Marian University	Fond du Lac	Wisconsin
Marshall University	Huntington	West Virginia
Martin Community College	Williamston	North Carolina
Martin Methodist College	Pulaski	Tennessee
Maryville University of Saint Louis	Saint Louis	Missouri
Massachusetts Bay Community College	Wellesley Hills	Massachusetts
Massachusetts Institute of Technology	Cambridge	Massachusetts
Mayville State University	Mayville	North Dakota
McKendree University	Lebanon	Illinois

Medaille College	Buffalo	New York
Menlo College	Athertono	California
Meramec Campus of St. Louis Community college	Kirkwood	Missouri
Mercer County Community College	Trenton	New Jersey
Metro Business College	Cape Girardeau	Missouri
Metropolitan Community College - Longview	Lee's Summit	Missouri
Metropolitan State University	St. Paul	Minnesota
Miami University Hamilton	Hamilton	Ohio
Michigan State University	East Lansing	Michigan
Michigan Technological University	Houghton	Michigan
Mid-America Christian University	Oklahoma City	Oklahoma
MidAmerica Nazarene University	Olathe	Kansas
Middlesex Community College	Middletown	Connecticut
Mid-South Community College	West Memphis	Arkansas
Midwestern State University	Wichita Falls	Texas
Millersville University of Pennsylvania	Millersville	Pennsylvania
Minnesota School of Business, Lakeville Campus	Lakeville	Minnesota
Minnesota State University, Mankato	Mankato	Minnesota
MiraCosta College	Oceanside	California
Misericordia University	Exeter	Pennsylvania
Mississippi Valley State University	Itta Bena	Mississippi
Missouri State University	Springfield	Missouri
Missouri Western State University	Saint Joseph	Missouri
Mitchell College	New London	Connecticut
Mitchell Technical Institute	Mitchell	South Dakota
Mohave Community College	Kingman	Arizona
Monmouth University	West Long Branch	New Jersey
Montclair State University	Montclair	New Jersey
Moraine Valley Community College	Palos Hills	Illinois
Morehead State University	Morehead	Kentucky
Morgan State University	Baltimore	Maryland
Mount Carmel College of Nursing	Columbus	Ohio
Mount Mary College	Milwaukee	Wisconsin
Mount St. Mary's University	Emmitsburg	Maryland
Mount Union College	Alliance	Ohio
Nashua Community College	Nashua	New Hampshire
Naugatuck Valley Community College	Waterbury	Connecticut
Navajo Technical College	Crownpoint	New Mexico
Nazareth College of Rochester	Rochester	New York
Nebraska Methodist College	Omaha	Nebraska

Neosho County Community College	Chanute	Kansas
Neumann University	Aston	Pennsylvania
New Mexico Junior College	Hobbs	New Mexico
New York Institute of Technology	New York City	New York
Newberry College	Newberry	South Carolina
Newman University	Wichita	Kansas
Niagara University	Lewiston	New York
Nicholls State University	Thibodaux	Louisiana
Nichols College	Dudley	Massachusetts
North Central State College	Mansfield	Ohio
North Dakota State College of Science	Wahpeton	North Dakota
North Georgia College and State University	Dahlonega	Georgia
North Hennepin Community College	Brooklyn Park	Minnesota
North Park University	Chicago	Illinois
Northeastern Oklahoma A&M College	Miami	Oklahoma
Northern Arizona University	Flagstaff	Arizona
Northern Illinois University	DeKalb	Illinois
Northern Maine Community College	Presque Isle	Maine
Northern Michigan University	Marquette	Michigan
Northern Wyoming Community College District	Sheridan	Wyoming
Northwest Missouri State University	Maryville	Missouri
Northwest State Community College	Archbold	Ohio
Northwestern Connecticut Community College	Winsted	Connecticut
Oak Hills Christian College	Bemidji	Minnesota
Oberlin College	Oberlin	Ohio
Occidental College	Los Angeles	California
Ohio University Zanesville	Zanesville	Ohio
Oregon College of Art and Craft	Portland	Oregon
Ouachita Technical College	Malvern	Arkansas
Our Lady of the Lake College	Baton Rouge	Louisiana
Our Lady of the Lake University	San Antonio	Texas
Ozarka College	Melbourne	Arkansas
Pacific Lutheran University	Tacoma	Washington
Paul Smith's College	Paul Smiths	New York
Pennsylvania School of Business	Allentown	Pennsylvania
Peru State College	Peru	Nebraska
Pfeiffer University	Misenheimer	North Carolina
Philadelphia University	Philadelphia	Pennsylvania
Piedmont Virginia Community College	Charlottesville	Virginia
Pikeville College	Pikeville	Kentucky

Pomona College	Claremont	California
Post University	Waterbury	Connecticut
Prairie State College	Chicago Heights	Illinois
Prince George's Community College	Largo	Maryland
Pulaski Technical College	North Little Rock	Arkansas
Purdue University	West Lafayette	Indiana
Radford University	Radford	Virginia
Reading Area Community College	Reading	Pennsylvania
Rider University	Lawrenceville	New Jersey
Robert Morris University	Moon Township	Pennsylvania
Roosevelt University	Chicago	Illinois
Rutgers University - Camden	Camden	New Jersey
Saint Joseph College	West Hartford	Connecticut
Saint Mary-of-the-Woods College	Saint Mary of the Woods	Indiana
Saint Michael's College	Colchester	Vermont
Saint Peter's College	Jersey City	New Jersey
Saint Xavier University	Chicago	Illinois
Sam Houston State University	Huntsville	Texas
San Francisco State University	San Francisco	California
Santa Rosa Junior College	Santa Rosa	California
Seattle University	Seattle	Washington
Seminole State College	Seminole	Oklahoma
Seton Hall University	South Orange	New Jersey
Shaw University	Raleigh	North Carolina
Shawnee State University	Portsmouth	Ohio
Shenandoah University	Winchester	Virginia
Shepherd University	Shepherdstown	West Virginia
Simmons College	Boston	Massachusetts
Simpson College	Indianola	Iowa
Simpson University	Redding	California
Skidmore College	Saratoga Springs	New York
Slippery Rock University of Pennsylvania	Slippery Rock	Pennsylvania
South Arkansas Community College	El Dorado	Arkansas
Southeast Missouri State University	Cape Girardeau	Missouri
Southeastern Bible College	Birmingham	Alabama
Southeastern Community College	Whiteville	North Carolina
Southeastern Louisiana University	Hammond	Louisiana
Southern Arkansas University	Magnolia	Arkansas
Southern Illinois University - Carbondale	Carbondale	Illinois

Southern Polytechnic State University	Marietta	Georgia
Southern University	Baton Rouge	Louisiana
Southern Vermont College	Bennington	Vermont
Southwestern Christian University	Bethay	Oklahoma
Southwestern Community College	Creston	Iowa
Southwestern Oklahoma State University	Weatherford	Oklahoma
Southwestern University	Georgetown	Texas
Spalding University	Louisville	Kentucky
Spartanburg Methodist College	Spartanburg	South Carolina
Spokane Falls Community College	Spokane	Washington
Spoon River College	Canton	Illinois
St. Elizabeth College of Nursing	Utica	New York
St. John Fisher College	Rochester	New York
St. Lawrence University	Canton	New York
St. Vincent's College	Bridgeport	Connecticut
Stark State College	North Canton	Ohio
Stephen F. Austin State University	Nacogdoches	Texas
Stephens College	Columbia	Missouri
Sterling College	Craftsbury Common	Vermont
Stetson University	DeLand	Florida
Stillman College	Tuscaloosa	Alabama
Sullivan College of Technology and Design	Louisville	Kentucky
Sullivan County Community College	Loch Sheldrake	New York
SUNY-College of Environmental Science and Forestry	Syracuse	New York
Sussex County Community College	Newton	New Jersey
Technical Career Institutes, Inc.	New York	New York
Texas A&M University	College Station	Texas
Texas A&M University - Corpus Christi	Corpus Christi	Texas
Texas A&M University - Kingsville	Kingsville	Texas
Texas Christian University	Fort Worth	Texas
Texas Southern University	Houston	Texas
Texas Woman's University	Denton	Texas
The Art Institute of California - San Francisco	San Francisco	California
The Art Institute of Houston	Houston	Texas
The Art Institute of Las Vegas	Las Vegas	Nevada
The College of Idaho	Caldwell	Idaho
The College of New Jersey	Ewing	New Jersey
The College of New Rochelle	New Rochelle	New York
The National Hispanic University	San Jose	California

The New England Institute of Art	Brookline	Massachusetts
The Pennsylvania State University	University Park	Pennsylvania
The Pennsylvania State University - DuBois Campus	DuBois	Pennsylvania
The Richard Stockton College of New Jersey	Pomona	New Jersey
The University of Montana	Missoula	Montana
The University of North Carolina at Greensboro	Greensboro	North Carolina
The University of Tampa	Tampa	Florida
The University of Texas at Dallas	Richardson	Texas
The University of Texas at El Paso	El Paso	Texas
The Victoria College	Victoria	Texas
Thomas College	Waterville	Maine
Thomas More College	Crestview Hills	Kentucky
Three Rivers Community College	Norwich	Connecticut
Tougaloo College	Tougaloo	Mississippi
Trine University	Angola	Indiana
Trinity Christian College	Palos Heights	Illinois
Trinity Western University	Langley	Washington
Tusculum College	Greeneville	Tennessee
Tuskegee University	Tuskegee	Alabama
Tyler Junior College	Tyler	Texas
Ulster County Community College	Stone Ridge	New York
Union College	Barbourville	Kentucky
Universidad del Turabo	Gurabo	Florida
University of Akron	Akron	Ohio
University of Arkansas Community College at Batesville	Batesville	Arkansas
University of Bridgeport	Bridgeport	Connecticut
University of Cincinnati	Cincinnati	Ohio
University of Cincinnati Clermont College	Batavia	Ohio
University of Dubuque	Dubuque	Iowa
University of Georgia	Athens	Georgia
University of Hawaii at Manoa	Honolulu	Hawaii
University of Massachusetts - Amherst	Amherst	Massachusetts
University of Memphis	Memphis	Tennessee
University of Minnesota	Minneapolis	Minnesota
University of Minnesota - Duluth	Duluth	Minnesota
University of Mississippi	University	Mississippi
University of Missouri - Kansas City	Kansas City	Missouri
University of Missouri - St. Louis	St. Louis	Missouri
University of New Hampshire	Durham	New Hampshire
University of New Hampshire at Manchester	Manchester	New Hampshire

University of New Mexico - Main Campus	Albuquerque	New Mexico
University of North Texas	Denton	Texas
University of Northern Colorado	Greeley	Colorado
University of Pittsburgh at Bradford	Bradford	Pennsylvania
University of Pittsburgh at Greensburg	Greensburg	Pennsylvania
University of Redlands	Redlands	California
University of Rhode Island	Kingston	Rhode Island
University of Richmond	Richmond	Virginia
University of Saint Francis	Fort Wayne	Indiana
University of South Alabama	Mobile	Alabama
University of South Carolina Aiken	Aiken	South Carolina
University of South Carolina Beaufort	Bluffton	South Carolina
University of South Carolina Columbia	Columbia	South Carolina
University South Carolina Union	Union	South Carolina
University of South Dakota	Vermillion	South Dakota
University of Tennessee - Martin	Martin	Tennessee
University of the Sciences in Philadelphia	Philadelphia	Pennsylvania
University of the Southwest	Hobbs	New Mexico
University of Toledo	Toledo	Ohio
University of Washington	Seattle	Washington
University of West Georgia	Carrollton	Georgia
University of Wisconsin - Eau Claire	Eau Claire	Wisconsin
University of Wisconsin - Madison	Madison	Wisconsin
University of Wisconsin - Parkside	Kenosha	Wisconsin
University of Wisconsin - Superior	Superior	Wisconsin
University of Wisconsin - Whitewater	Whitewater	Wisconsin
Utah State University	Logan	Utah
Utica School of Commerce	Utica	New York
Valdosta State University	Valdosta	Georgia
Valencia Community College	Orlando	Florida
Vassar College	Poughkeepsie	New York
Villanova University	Villanova	Pennsylvania
Virginia College School of Business and Health	Chattanooga	Tennessee
Virginia Commonwealth University	Richmond	Virginia
Virginia Intermont College	Bristol	Virginia
Virginia State University	Petersburg	Virginia
Voorhees College	Denmark	South Carolina
Wake Forest University	Winston-Salem	North Carolina
Waldorf College	Forest City	Iowa
Walsh University	North Canton	Ohio

Appendix D: Comprehensive Frequency Distribution Tables for the 2009 National Survey of First-Year Seminars

All Responses by Institutional Type, Control, and Size

Item	Survey question	Two-year		Four-year		Public		Private		FY class size less than 500		FY class size 501 - 1,000		FY class size 1,001 - 2,000		FY class size 2,001 - 3,000		FY class size 3,001 - 4,000		FY class size 4,001+		Total	
		n	%	n	%	n	%	n	%	n	%	n	%	n	%	n	%	n	%	n	%	n	%
Q9	Does your institution offer one or more first-year seminar-type courses?																						
	I don't know	1	0.3	1	0.1	1	0.2	1	0.2	0	0.0	0	0.0	1	0.5	1	1.2	0	0.0	0	0.0	2	0.2
	No	57	19.5	70	9.6	64	12.1	63	12.9	60	16.4	28	11.8	16	8.3	12	13.8	4	6.9	7	9.1	127	12.5
	Yes	235	80.2	655	90.2	464	87.7	426	86.9	305	83.6	210	88.2	177	91.2	74	85.1	54	93.1	70	90.9	890	87.3
	Total	293	100.0	726	100.0	529	100.0	490	100.0	365	100.0	238	100.0	194	100.0	87	100.0	58	100.0	77	100.0	1019	100.0
Q10	Percentage of first-year students who take a first-year seminar course																						
	Less than 10%	47	20.5	20	3.1	62	13.6	5	1.2	6	2.0	13	6.3	16	9.1	8	11.0	11	20.8	13	19.4	67	7.6
	10% - 19%	32	14.0	27	4.2	52	11.4	7	1.7	5	1.7	15	7.2	15	8.5	8	11.0	11	20.8	5	7.5	59	6.7
	20% - 29%	25	10.9	35	5.4	52	11.4	8	1.9	8	2.6	12	5.8	16	9.1	10	13.7	4	7.5	10	14.9	60	6.8
	30% - 39%	17	7.4	37	5.7	38	8.3	16	3.8	11	3.6	10	4.8	10	5.7	6	8.2	2	3.8	15	22.4	54	6.1
	40% - 49%	7	3.1	14	2.2	13	2.9	8	1.9	7	2.3	3	1.4	6	3.4	2	2.7	2	3.8	1	1.5	21	2.4
	50% - 59%	8	3.5	24	3.7	27	5.9	5	1.2	2	1.0	7	3.4	10	5.7	5	6.8	2	3.8	6	9.0	32	3.6
	60% - 69%	7	3.1	18	2.8	18	3.9	7	1.7	3	1.0	3	1.4	7	4.0	3	4.1	3	5.7	6	9.0	25	2.8
	70% - 79%	15	6.6	28	4.3	33	7.2	10	2.4	9	3.0	11	5.3	11	6.3	7	9.6	3	5.7	2	3.0	43	4.9
	80% - 89%	22	9.6	44	6.8	41	9.0	25	5.9	21	7.0	14	6.7	18	10.2	6	8.2	5	9.4	2	3.0	66	7.5

Table continues p. 100

Table continued from p. 99

Item	Survey question	Two-year n	%	Four-year n	%	Public n	%	Private n	%	FY class size less than 500 n	%	FY class size 501 - 1,000 n	%	FY class size 1,001 - 2,000 n	%	FY class size 2,001 - 3,000 n	%	FY class size 3,001 - 4,000 n	%	FY class size 4,001+ n	%	Total n	%
Q10	Percentage of first-year students who take a first-year seminar course *(continued)*																						
	90% - 99%	30	13.1	152	23.4	72	15.8	110	26.0	84	27.8	52	25.0	29	16.5	12	16.4	2	3.8	3	4.5	182	20.7
	100%	19	8.3	251	38.6	48	10.5	222	52.5	146	48.3	68	32.7	38	21.6	6	8.2	8	15.1	4	6.0	270	30.7
	Total	229	100.0	650	100.0	456	100.0	423	100.0	302	100.0	208	100.0	176	100.0	73	100.0	53	100.0	67	100.0	879	100.0
Q11	Years a first-year seminar offered on campus?																						
	Two years or less	58	25.3	63	9.7	76	16.7	45	10.6	43	14.2	33	15.9	17	9.7	8	11.0	11	20.8	9	13.4	121	13.8
	Three to 10 years	106	46.3	272	41.8	196	43.0	182	43.0	133	44.0	90	43.3	80	45.5	26	35.6	21	39.6	28	41.8	378	43.0
	More than 10 years	65	28.4	315	48.5	184	40.4	196	46.3	126	41.7	85	40.9	79	44.1	39	53.4	21	39.6	30	44.8	380	43.2
	Total	229	100.0	650	100.0	456	100.0	423	100.0	302	100.0	208	100.0	176	100.0	73	100.0	53	100.0	67	100.0	879	100.0
Q12	Select each discrete type of first-year seminar that exist on your campus: (Check all that apply)																						
	Extended orientation seminar	176	74.9	373	57.0	330	71.1	219	51.4	169	55.4	121	57.6	122	68.9	50	67.6	35	64.8	52	74.3	549	61.7
	Academic seminar with uniform academic content	52	22.1	178	27.2	118	25.4	112	26.3	87	28.5	52	24.8	47	26.6	16	21.6	10	18.5	18	25.7	230	25.8
	Academic seminar on various topics	14	6.0	194	29.6	83	17.9	125	29.3	70	23.0	53	25.2	38	21.5	10	13.5	13	24.1	24	34.3	208	23.4
	Preprofessional or discipline-linked seminar	22	9.4	106	16.2	87	18.8	41	9.6	23	7.5	35	16.7	26	14.7	12	16.2	10	18.5	22	31.4	128	14.4

Item	Survey question	Two-year n	%	Four-year n	%	Public n	%	Private n	%	FY class size less than 500 n	%	FY class size 501-1,000 n	%	FY class size 1,001-2,000 n	%	FY class size 2,001-3,000 n	%	FY class size 3,001-4,000 n	%	FY class size 4,001+ n	%	Total n	%
Q12	Select each discrete type of first-year seminar that exist on your campus: Check all that apply (continued)																						
	Basic study skills seminar	92	39.2	107	16.3	139	30.0	60	14.1	49	16.1	37	17.6	42	23.7	28	37.8	18	33.3	25	35.7	199	22.4
	Hybrid	42	17.9	157	24.0	99	21.3	100	23.5	79	25.9	39	18.6	32	18.1	16	21.6	15	27.8	18	25.7	199	22.4
	Other	9	3.8	13	2.0	14	3.0	8	1.9	8	2.6	5	2.4	4	2.3	0	0.0	1	1.9	4	5.7	22	2.5
Q15	If more than one first-year seminar type, the type with the highest total student enrollment:																						
	Extended orientation seminar	116	52.0	238	37.2	223	49.9	131	31.6	100	33.7	80	39.4	77	44.8	38	53.5	24	46.2	35	52.2	354	41.1
	Academic seminar with uniform academic content	33	14.8	106	16.6	61	13.6	78	18.8	51	17.2	37	18.2	29	16.9	11	15.5	6	11.5	5	7.5	139	16.1
	Academic seminar on various topics	6	2.7	127	19.9	42	9.4	91	21.9	47	15.8	38	18.7	22	12.8	6	8.5	8	15.4	12	17.9	133	15.4
	Preprofessional or discipline-linked seminar	4	1.8	28	4.4	19	4.3	13	3.1	5	1.7	12	5.9	8	4.7	0	0.0	3	5.8	4	6.0	32	3.7
	Basic study skills seminar	29	13.0	13	2.0	35	7.8	7	1.7	8	2.7	7	3.4	13	7.6	6	8.5	3	5.8	5	7.5	42	4.9
	Hybrid	26	11.7	106	16.6	51	11.4	81	19.5	68	22.9	26	12.8	19	11.0	9	12.7	6	11.5	4	6.0	132	15.3
	Other	9	4.0	21	3.3	16	3.6	14	3.4	18	6.1	3	1.5	4	2.3	1	1.4	2	3.8	2	3.0	30	3.5
	Total	223	100.0	639	100.0	447	100.0	415	100.0	297	100.0	203	100.0	172	100.0	71	100.0	52	100.0	67	100.0	862	100.0

Table continues p. 102

Table continued from p. 101

Item	Survey question	Two-year		Four-year		Public		Private		FY class size less than 500		FY class size 501 - 1,000		FY class size 1,001 - 2,000		FY class size 2,001 - 3,000		FY class size 3,001 - 4,000		FY class size 4,001+		Total	
		n	%	n	%	n	%	n	%	n	%	n	%	n	%	n	%	n	%	n	%	n	%
Q16	Approximate number of sections seminar type will be offered in the 2009/2010 academic year:																						
	0	0	0.0	0	0.0	0	0.0	0	0.0	0	0.0	0	0.0	0	0.0	0	0.0	0	0.0	0	0.0	0	0.0
	1 - 10	76	34.1	141	22.1	110	24.6	107	25.8	112	37.7	45	22.2	30	17.4	13	18.3	10	19.2	7	10.4	217	25.2
	11 - 20	62	27.8	180	28.2	110	24.6	132	31.8	120	40.4	56	27.6	31	18.0	11	15.5	14	26.9	10	14.9	242	28.1
	21 - 30	26	11.7	119	18.6	62	13.9	83	20.0	56	18.9	41	20.2	26	15.1	11	15.5	2	3.8	9	13.4	145	16.8
	31 - 40	18	8.1	49	7.7	35	7.8	32	7.7	3	1.0	32	15.8	15	8.7	8	11.3	5	9.6	4	6.0	67	7.8
	41 - 50	9	4.0	41	6.4	29	6.5	21	5.1	1	0.3	16	7.9	19	11.0	3	4.2	4	7.7	7	10.4	50	5.8
	51 - 60	7	3.1	24	3.8	22	4.9	9	2.2	3	1.0	3	1.5	16	9.3	4	5.6	1	1.9	4	6.0	31	3.6
	61 - 70	4	1.8	22	3.4	20	4.5	6	1.4	0	0.0	4	2.0	14	8.1	5	7.0	0	0.0	3	4.5	26	3.0
	71 - 80	4	1.8	11	1.7	11	2.4	4	1.0	0	0.0	1	0.5	8	4.7	3	4.2	1	1.9	2	3.0	15	1.7
	81 - 90	3	1.3	8	1.3	11	2.4	0	0.0	0	0.0	1	0.5	4	2.3	2	2.8	1	1.9	3	4.5	11	1.3
	91 - 100	1	0.4	10	1.6	9	2.0	2	0.5	0	0.0	1	0.5	4	2.3	2	2.8	1	5.8	1	1.5	11	1.3
	Over 100	13	5.8	34	5.3	28	6.3	19	4.6	2	0.7	3	1.5	5	2.9	9	12.7	3	21.2	17	25.4	47	5.5
	Total	223	100.0	639	100.0	447	100.0	415	100.0	297	100.0	203	100.0	172	100.0	71	100.0	52	100.0	67	100.0	862	100.0
Q17	Approximate class size for each first-year seminar section?																						
	10 students or fewer	4	1.8	9	1.4	3	0.7	10	2.4	10	3.4	1	0.5	2	1.2	0	0.0	0	0.0	0	0.0	13	1.5
	11 - 15	24	10.9	113	17.8	44	10.0	93	22.5	66	22.4	40	19.7	18	10.5	3	4.2	5	9.6	5	7.8	137	16.0
	16 - 19	29	13.1	187	29.5	62	14.1	154	37.2	102	34.7	53	26.1	37	21.6	9	12.7	4	7.7	11	17.2	216	25.3
	20 - 24	92	41.6	190	30.0	193	43.8	89	21.5	69	23.5	59	29.1	67	39.2	28	39.4	25	48.1	34	53.1	282	33.0

Item	Survey question	Two-year		Four-year		Public		Private		FY class size less than 500		FY class size 501 - 1,000		FY class size 1,001 - 2,000		FY class size 2,001 - 3,000		FY class size 3,001 - 4,000		FY class size 4,001+		Total	
		n	%	n	%	n	%	n	%	n	%	n	%	n	%	n	%	n	%	n	%	n	%
Q17	Approximate class size for each first-year seminar section? (*continued*)																						
	25 - 29	51	23.1	83	13.1	96	21.8	38	9.2	28	9.5	29	14.3	31	18.1	22	31.0	13	25.0	11	17.2	134	15.7
	30 or more	21	9.5	52	8.2	43	9.8	30	7.2	19	6.5	21	10.3	16	9.4	9	12.7	5	9.6	3	4.7	73	8.5
	Total	221	100.0	634	100.0	441	100.0	414	100.0	294	100.0	203	100.0	171	100.0	71	100.0	52	100.0	64	100.0	855	100.0
Q18	Approximate percentage of first-year students required to take the first-year seminar?																						
	None	73	33.0	95	15.0	129	29.3	39	9.4	23	7.8	43	21.2	38	22.2	19	26.8	25	48.1	20	31.3	168	19.6
	Less than 10%	20	9.0	37	5.8	50	11.3	7	1.7	5	1.7	8	3.9	17	9.9	11	15.5	4	7.7	12	18.8	57	6.7
	10% - 19%	11	5.0	27	4.3	31	7.0	7	1.7	7	2.4	6	3.0	9	5.3	6	8.5	4	7.7	6	9.4	38	4.4
	20% - 29%	9	4.1	16	2.5	23	5.2	2	0.5	3	1.0	5	2.5	8	4.7	2	2.8	0	0.0	7	10.9	25	2.9
	30% - 39%	9	4.1	9	1.4	14	3.2	4	1.0	4	1.4	2	1.0	2	1.2	4	5.6	3	5.8	3	4.7	18	2.1
	40% - 49%	2	1.0	8	1.3	8	1.8	2	0.5	0	0.0	2	1.0	5	2.9	0	0.0	2	3.8	1	1.6	10	1.2
	50% - 59%	5	2.3	5	1.0	7	1.6	3	0.7	2	0.7	2	1.0	3	1.8	0	0.0	0	0.0	3	4.7	10	1.2
	60% - 69%	3	1.4	10	1.6	10	2.3	3	0.7	2	0.7	3	1.5	4	2.3	2	2.8	0	0.0	2	3.1	13	1.5
	70% - 79%	9	4.1	11	1.7	12	2.7	8	1.9	6	2.0	6	3.0	5	2.9	1	1.4	1	1.9	1	1.6	20	2.3
	80% - 89%	11	5.0	16	2.5	15	3.4	12	2.9	8	2.7	3	1.5	11	6.4	4	5.6	1	1.9	0	0.0	27	3.2
	90% - 99%	26	11.8	104	16.4	50	11.3	80	19.3	71	24.1	28	13.8	20	11.7	6	8.5	2	3.8	3	4.7	130	15.2
	100%	43	19.5	296	46.7	92	20.9	247	59.7	163	55.4	95	46.8	49	28.7	16	22.5	10	19.2	6	9.4	339	39.6
	Total	221	100.0	634	100.0	441	100.0	414	100.0	294	100.0	203	100.0	171	100.0	71	100.0	52	100.0	64	100.0	855	100.0

Table continues p. 104

Table continued from p. 103

Item	Survey question	Two-year		Four-year		Public		Private		FY class size less than 500		FY class size 501 - 1,000		FY class size 1,001 - 2,000		FY class size 2,001 - 3,000		FY class size 3,001 - 4,000		FY class size 4,001+		Total	
		n	%	n	%	n	%	n	%	n	%	n	%	n	%	n	%	n	%	n	%	n	%
Q19	Which students, by category, are required to take the first-year seminar?																						
	None are required to take it	71	30.2	90	13.7	122	26.3	39	9.2	23	7.5	40	19.1	38	21.5	18	24.3	23	42.6	19	27.1	161	18.1
	All first-year students are required to take it	74	31.5	407	62.1	146	31.5	335	78.6	241	79.0	123	58.6	73	41.2	24	32.4	11	20.4	9	12.9	481	54.0
	Academically underprepared students	43	18.3	85	13.0	88	19.0	40	9.4	35	11.5	23	11.0	36	20.3	11	14.9	6	11.1	17	24.3	128	14.4
	First-generation students	6	2.6	39	6.0	14	3.0	31	7.3	22	7.2	10	4.8	7	4.0	2	2.7	2	3.7	2	2.9	45	5.1
	Honors students	5	2.1	51	7.8	28	6.0	28	6.6	18	5.9	11	5.2	12	6.8	3	4.1	5	9.3	7	10.0	56	6.3
	International students	4	1.7	31	4.7	11	2.4	24	5.6	16	5.3	7	3.3	8	4.5	2	2.7	1	1.9	1	1.4	35	3.9
	Learning community participants	9	3.8	55	8.4	38	8.2	26	6.1	21	6.9	9	4.3	13	7.3	6	8.1	9	16.7	6	8.6	64	7.2
	Preprofessional students	2	0.9	25	3.8	8	1.7	19	4.5	12	3.9	7	3.3	7	4.0	0	0.0	1	1.9	0	0.0	27	3.0
	Provisionally admitted students	3	1.3	59	9.0	35	7.5	27	6.3	20	6.6	15	7.1	16	9.0	5	6.8	2	3.7	4	5.7	62	7.0
	Student-athletes	9	3.8	56	8.6	36	7.8	29	6.8	21	6.8	10	6.9	10	4.8	11	14.9	5	14.9	8	11.4	65	7.3

Item	Survey question	Two-year		Four-year		Public		Private		FY class size less than 500		FY class size 501 - 1,000		FY class size 1,001 - 2,000		FY class size 2,001 - 3,000		FY class size 3,001 - 4,000		FY class size 4,001+		Total	
		n	%	n	%	n	%	n	%	n	%	n	%	n	%	n	%	n	%	n	%	n	%
Q19	*Which students, by category, are required to take the first-year seminar? (continued)*																						
	Students participating in dual-enrollment programs	3	1.3	12	1.8	7	1.5	8	1.9	6	2.0	3	1.4	4	2.3	0	0.0	2	3.7	0	0.0	15	1.7
	Students residing within a particular residence hall	1	0.4	19	2.9	12	2.6	8	1.9	7	2.3	2	1.0	5	2.8	2	2.7	1	1.9	3	4.3	20	2.3
	Students within specific majors	20	8.5	32	4.9	38	8.2	14	3.3	6	2.0	8	3.8	22	12.4	4	5.4	5	9.3	7	10.0	52	5.8
	Transfer students	7	3.0	39	6.0	12	2.6	34	8.0	25	8.2	8	3.8	8	4.5	2	2.7	0	0.0	3	4.3	46	5.2
	TRIO participants	11	4.7	24	3.7	29	6.3	6	1.4	8	2.6	4	1.9	7	4.0	4	5.4	4	7.4	8	11.4	35	3.9
	Undeclared students	3	1.3	38	5.8	17	3.7	24	5.6	16	5.3	9	4.3	10	5.7	2	2.7	2	3.7	2	2.9	41	4.6
	Other (please specify)	35	14.9	64	9.8	61	13.2	38	8.9	24	7.9	20	9.5	23	13.0	11	14.9	7	13.0	14	20.0	99	11.1
Q20	Please identify unique subpopulations of students for which special sections of the first-year seminar are offered:																						
	No special sections are offered	104	44.3	277	42.3	160	34.5	221	51.9	157	51.5	107	51.0	56	31.6	26	35.1	21	38.9	14	20.0	381	42.8
	Academically underprepared students	50	21.3	104	15.9	96	20.7	58	13.6	44	14.4	31	14.8	36	20.3	11	14.9	10	18.5	22	31.4	154	17.3
	First-generation students	10	4.3	16	2.4	19	4.1	7	1.6	7	2.3	3	1.4	4	2.3	2	2.7	3	5.6	7	10.0	26	2.9
	Honors students	12	5.1	160	24.4	83	17.9	89	20.9	58	19.0	31	14.8	39	22.0	18	24.3	10	18.5	16	22.9	172	19.3

Table continues p. 106

Table continued from p. 105

Item	Survey question	Two-year		Four-year		Public		Private		FY class size less than 500		FY class size 501 - 1,000		FY class size 1,001 - 2,000		FY class size 2,001 - 3,000		FY class size 3,001 - 4,000		FY class size 4,001+		Total	
		n	%	n	%	n	%	n	%	n	%	n	%	n	%	n	%	n	%	n	%	n	%
Q20	Please identify unique subpopulations of students for which special sections of the first-year seminar are offered: *(continued)*																						
	International students	9	3.8	26	4.0	23	5.0	12	2.8	8	2.6	8	3.8	4	4.5	2	5.4	2	3.7	5	7.1	35	3.9
	Learning community participants	46	19.6	109	16.6	120	25.9	35	8.2	19	6.2	33	15.7	31	17.5	22	29.7	23	42.6	27	38.6	155	17.4
	Preprofessional students (e.g., prelaw, premed)	4	1.7	41	6.3	33	7.1	12	2.8	9	3.0	12	5.7	7	4.0	5	6.8	6	11.1	6	8.6	45	5.1
	Provisionally admitted students	1	0.4	34	5.2	24	5.2	11	2.6	9	3.0	5	2.4	7	4.0	7	9.5	2	3.7	5	7.1	35	3.9
	Student-athletes	13	5.5	54	8.2	58	12.5	9	2.1	5	1.6	12	5.7	18	10.2	14	18.9	6	11.1	12	17.1	67	7.5
	Students participating in dual-enrollment programs	10	4.3	5	0.8	14	3.0	1	0.2	3	1.0	1	0.5	2	1.1	1	1.4	4	7.4	4	5.7	15	1.7
	Students residing within a particular residence hall	0	0.0	28	4.3	21	4.5	7	1.6	3	1.0	4	1.9	4	2.3	6	8.1	2	3.7	9	12.9	28	3.2
	Students within specific majors	21	8.9	95	14.5	83	17.9	33	7.8	25	8.2	22	10.5	32	18.1	15	20.3	9	16.7	13	18.6	116	13.0
	Transfer students	4	1.7	47	7.2	26	5.6	25	5.9	16	5.3	6	2.9	13	7.3	3	4.1	5	9.3	8	11.4	51	5.7
	TRIO participants	13	5.5	28	4.3	37	8.0	4	0.9	5	1.6	6	2.9	11	6.2	6	8.1	3	5.6	10	14.3	41	4.6

Item	Survey question	Two-year		Four-year		Public		Private		FY class size less than 500		FY class size 501 - 1,000		FY class size 1,001 - 2,000		FY class size 2,001 - 3,000		FY class size 3,001 - 4,000		FY class size 4,001+		Total	
		n	%	n	%	n	%	n	%	n	%	n	%	n	%	n	%	n	%	n	%	n	%
Q20	Please identify unique sub-populations of students for which special sections of the first-year seminar are offered: *(continued)*																						
	Undeclared students	5	2.1	51	7.8	43	9.3	13	3.1	7	2.3	14	6.7	14	7.9	10	13.5	3	5.6	8	11.4	56	6.3
	Other (please specify)	26	11.1	55	8.4	54	11.6	27	6.3	17	5.6	17	8.1	18	10.2	13	17.6	4	7.4	12	17.1	81	9.1
Q21	Who teaches the first-year seminar?																						
	Adjunct faculty	145	61.7	264	40.3	255	55.0	154	36.2	108	35.4	88	41.9	99	55.9	44	59.5	27	50.0	43	61.4	409	46.0
	Full-time non-tenure-track faculty	108	46.0	376	57.4	235	50.7	249	58.5	161	52.8	126	60.0	103	58.2	36	48.7	27	50.0	31	44.3	484	54.4
	Graduate students	1	0.4	49	7.5	37	8.0	13	3.1	4	1.3	9	4.3	14	7.9	9	12.2	6	11.1	8	11.4	50	5.6
	Student affairs professionals	106	45.1	323	49.3	244	52.6	185	43.4	132	43.3	99	47.1	82	46.3	44	59.5	34	63.0	38	54.3	429	48.2
	Tenure-track faculty	98	41.7	448	68.4	266	57.3	280	65.7	183	60.0	130	61.9	116	65.5	36	48.7	34	63.0	47	67.1	546	61.4
	Undergraduate students	0	0.0	45	6.9	17	3.7	28	6.6	17	5.6	10	4.8	5	2.8	2	2.7	3	5.6	8	11.4	45	5.1
	Other campus professionals	56	23.8	210	32.1	142	30.6	124	29.1	86	28.2	66	31.4	54	30.5	25	33.8	15	27.8	20	28.6	266	29.9
Q22	If undergraduate students assist in the first-year seminar, what is their role?																						
	They teach independently	0	0.0	13	28.9	7	41.2	6	21.4	1	5.9	5	50.0	2	40.0	1	50.0	2	66.7	2	25.0	13	28.9
	They teach as a part of a team	0	0.0	31	68.9	10	58.8	21	75.0	12	70.6	7	70.6	3	60.0	1	50.0	1	33.3	7	87.5	31	68.9

Table continues p. 108

Table continued from p. 107

Item	Survey question	Two-year n	Two-year %	Four-year n	Four-year %	Public n	Public %	Private n	Private %	FY class size less than 500 n	%	FY class size 501-1,000 n	%	FY class size 1,001-2,000 n	%	FY class size 2,001-3,000 n	%	FY class size 3,001-4,000 n	%	FY class size 4,001+ n	%	Total n	%
Q22	If undergraduate students assist in the first-year seminar, what is their role? *(continued)*																						
	They assist the instructor, but do not teach	0	0.0	10	22.2	4	23.5	6	21.4	4	23.5	3	30.0	1	30.0	0	20.0	1	0.0	1	33.3	10	22.2
	Other (please specify)	0	0.0	7	15.6	3	17.6	4	14.3	2	11.8	3	30.0	0	0.0	.	0.0	2	66.7	0	0.0	7	15.6
Q23	Approximate percentage of sections that are team taught																						
	No sections	140	63.9	341	53.8	245	55.8	236	57.0	172	58.5	121	59.6	98	57.3	39	55.7	23	45.1	28	43.8	481	56.4
	Less than 10%	42	19.2	145	22.9	99	22.6	88	21.3	52	17.7	45	22.2	43	25.1	13	18.6	14	27.5	20	31.3	187	21.9
	10% - 19%	8	3.7	30	4.7	27	6.2	11	2.7	11	3.7	6	3.0	8	4.7	6	8.6	2	3.9	5	7.8	38	4.5
	20% - 29%	5	2.3	11	1.7	10	2.3	6	1.4	3	1.0	5	2.5	2	1.2	3	4.3	1	2.0	2	3.1	16	1.9
	30% - 39%	3	1.4	11	1.7	8	1.8	6	1.4	7	2.4	1	0.5	4	2.3	1	1.4	1	2.0	0	0.0	14	1.6
	40% - 49%	1	0.5	1	0.2	2	0.5	0	0.0	0	0.0	0	0.0	1	0.6	0	0.0	1	2.0	0	0.0	2	0.2
	50% - 59%	4	1.8	12	1.9	5	1.1	11	2.7	7	2.4	3	2.4	2	1.5	1	1.2	1	2.0	2	3.1	16	1.9
	60% - 69%	1	0.5	1	0.2	1	0.2	1	0.2	1	0.3	1	0.5	0	0.5	0	0.0	0	0.0	0	0.0	2	0.2
	70% - 79%	0	0.0	6	0.9	3	0.7	3	0.7	2	0.7	1	0.5	1	0.5	0	0.0	2	3.9	0	0.0	6	0.7
	80% - 89%	1	0.5	2	0.3	3	0.7	0	0.0	0	0.0	0	0.0	1	0.0	0	0.6	1	0.0	1	2.0	3	0.4
	90% - 99%	4	1.8	11	1.8	8	1.8	7	1.7	10	1.7	1	0.5	2	0.5	1	1.2	1	1.4	0	2.0	15	1.8
	100%	10	4.6	63	9.9	28	6.4	45	10.9	29	9.9	19	9.4	9	9.4	6	8.6	4	7.8	6	9.4	73	8.6
	Total	219	100.0	634	100.0	439	100.0	414	100.0	294	100.0	203	100.0	171	100.0	70	100.0	51	100.0	64	100.0	853	100.0

Item	Survey question	Two-year n	Two-year %	Four-year n	Four-year %	Public n	Public %	Private n	Private %	FY class size less than 500 n	FY class size less than 500 %	FY class size 501-1,000 n	FY class size 501-1,000 %	FY class size 1,001-2,000 n	FY class size 1,001-2,000 %	FY class size 2,001-3,000 n	FY class size 2,001-3,000 %	FY class size 3,001-4,000 n	FY class size 3,001-4,000 %	FY class size 4,001+ n	FY class size 4,001+ %	Total n	Total %
Q25	Are any first-year students intentionally placed in sections taught by their academic advisors?																						
	I don't know	23	10.5	45	7.1	43	9.8	25	6.1	20	6.8	19	9.4	14	8.2	7	10.0	3	5.9	5	7.8	68	8.0
	No	153	69.9	365	57.7	276	62.9	242	58.6	173	58.8	126	62.1	100	58.8	44	62.9	32	62.7	43	67.2	518	60.8
	Yes	43	19.6	223	35.2	120	27.3	146	35.4	101	34.4	58	28.6	56	32.9	19	27.1	16	31.4	16	25.0	266	31.2
	Total	219	100.0	633	100.0	439	100.0	413	100.0	294	100.0	203	100.0	170	100.0	70	100.0	51	100.0	64	100.0	852	100.0
Q26	Approximate percentage of students placed in sections with their academic advisors?																						
	Less than 10%	15	34.9	32	14.3	29	24.2	18	12.3	15	14.9	9	15.5	10	17.9	3	15.8	6	37.5	4	25.0	47	17.7
	10% - 19%	7	16.3	25	11.2	23	19.2	9	6.2	8	7.8	5	8.6	10	17.9	5	26.3	4	25.0	0	0.0	32	12.0
	20% - 29%	8	18.6	20	9.0	21	17.5	7	4.8	3	3.0	6	10.3	8	14.3	4	21.1	3	18.8	4	25.0	28	10.5
	30% - 39%	3	7.0	13	5.8	11	9.2	5	3.4	4	4.0	4	6.9	2	3.6	2	10.5	1	6.3	3	18.8	16	6.0
	40% - 49%	2	4.7	12	5.4	9	7.5	5	3.4	6	5.9	2	3.4	4	7.1	0	0.0	0	0.0	2	12.5	14	5.3
	50% - 59%	2	4.7	12	5.4	6	5.0	8	5.5	4	4.0	6	10.3	2	3.6	2	10.5	0	0.0	0	0.0	14	5.3
	60% - 69%	2	4.7	6	2.7	5	4.2	3	2.1	3	3.0	0	0.0	3	5.4	1	5.3	0	0.0	1	6.3	8	3.0
	70% - 79%	0	0.0	5	2.2	1	0.8	2	2.7	2	2.0	2	3.4	1	1.8	0	0.0	0	0.0	0	0.0	5	1.9
	80% - 89%	0	0.0	7	3.1	3	2.5	4	2.7	3	3.0	1	1.7	1	1.8	0	0.0	1	6.3	1	6.3	7	2.6
	90% - 99%	1	2.3	17	7.6	6	5.0	12	8.2	11	10.9	3	5.2	2	3.6	1	5.3	0	0.0	1	6.3	18	6.8
	100%	3	7.0	74	33.2	6	5.0	71	48.6	42	41.6	20	34.5	13	23.2	1	5.3	1	6.3	0	0.0	77	28.9
	Total	43	100.0	223	100.0	120	100.0	146	100.0	101	100.0	58	100.0	56	100.0	19	100.0	16	100.0	16	100.0	266	100.0

Table continues p. 110

Table continued from p. 109

Item	Survey question	Two-year n	Two-year %	Four-year n	Four-year %	Public n	Public %	Private n	Private %	FY class size less than 500 n	FY class size less than 500 %	FY class size 501-1,000 n	FY class size 501-1,000 %	FY class size 1,001-2,000 n	FY class size 1,001-2,000 %	FY class size 2,001-3,000 n	FY class size 2,001-3,000 %	FY class size 3,001-4,000 n	FY class size 3,001-4,000 %	FY class size 4,001+ n	FY class size 4,001+ %	Total n	Total %
Q27	Faculty who teach the first-year seminar teach the course as:																						
	An overload course	57	58.2	217	48.4	151	56.8	123	43.9	88	48.1	60	46.2	58	50.0	21	58.3	19	55.9	28	59.6	274	50.2
	Part of regular teaching load	75	76.5	293	65.4	176	66.2	192	68.6	126	68.9	92	70.8	78	67.2	20	55.6	21	61.8	31	66.0	368	67.4
	Other (please specify)	5	5.1	56	12.5	35	13.2	26	9.3	18	9.8	10	7.7	15	12.9	5	13.9	4	11.8	9	19.1	61	11.2
Q28	Graduate students who teach the first-year seminar teach the course as:																						
	An assigned responsibility	0	0.0	26	53.1	22	59.5	4	30.8	1	25.0	3	33.3	7	50.0	5	55.6	4	66.7	6	75.0	26	52.0
	An extra responsibility	1	100.0	21	42.9	14	37.8	8	61.5	2	50.0	6	66.7	5	35.7	3	33.3	2	33.3	4	50.0	22	44.0
	Other (please specify)	0	0.0	10	20.4	9	24.3	1	7.7	1	25.0	0	0.0	3	21.4	3	33.3	0	0.0	3	37.5	10	20.0
Q29	Student affairs professionals who teach the first-year seminar teach the course as:																						
	An assigned responsibility	39	36.8	88	27.2	82	33.6	45	24.3	34	25.8	24	24.2	26	31.7	14	31.8	11	32.4	18	47.4	127	29.6
	An extra responsibility	69	65.1	246	76.2	177	48.0	138	74.6	99	75.0	75	75.8	63	76.8	32	72.7	22	64.7	24	63.2	315	73.4
	Other (please specify)	13	12.3	43	13.3	33	13.5	23	12.4	9	6.8	16	16.2	13	15.9	8	18.2	5	14.7	5	13.2	56	13.1

Item	Survey question	Two-year		Four-year		Public		Private		FY class size less than 500		FY class size 501–1,000		FY class size 1,001–2,000		FY class size 2,001–3,000		FY class size 3,001–4,000		FY class size 4,001+		Total	
		n	%	n	%	n	%	n	%	n	%	n	%	n	%	n	%	n	%	n	%	n	%
Q30	Type of compensation is offered to adjunct faculty for teaching the first-year seminar?																						
	No compensation is offered	20	13.8	36	13.6	37	14.5	19	12.3	8	7.4	13	14.8	14	14.1	6	13.6	5	18.5	10	23.3	56	13.7
	Graduate student support	0	0.0	2	0.8	2	0.8	0	0.0	0	0.0	0	0.0	0	0.0	0	0.0	1	3.7	1	2.3	2	0.5
	Release time	4	2.8	4	1.5	6	2.4	2	1.3	2	1.9	0	0.0	3	3.0	2	4.5	0	0.0	1	2.3	8	2.0
	Stipend	56	38.6	159	60.2	127	49.8	88	57.1	68	63.0	44	50.0	54	54.5	19	43.2	14	51.9	16	37.2	215	52.6
	Unrestricted professional development funds	2	1.4	4	1.5	6	2.4	0	0.0	1	0.9	0	0.0	0	0.0	1	2.2	1	3.7	3	7.0	6	1.5
	Other (please specify)	70	48.3	74	28.0	94	36.9	50	32.5	33	30.6	32	36.4	33	33.3	20	45.5	10	37.0	16	37.2	144	35.2
Q31	Type of compensation is offered to tenure faculty for teaching the first-year seminar?																						
	No compensation is offered	32	32.7	163	36.4	91	34.2	104	37.1	59	37.1	55	32.2	40	42.3	15	41.7	8	23.5	18	38.3	195	35.7
	Graduate student support	0	0.0	2	0.4	1	0.4	1	0.4	0	0.0	0	0.0	1	0.9	0	0.0	1	2.9	0	0.0	2	0.4
	Release time	4	4.1	24	5.4	16	6.0	12	4.3	9	4.9	5	4.9	7	6.0	2	5.6	2	5.9	3	6.4	28	5.1
	Stipend	23	23.5	180	40.2	87	32.7	116	41.4	81	44.3	43	44.3	38	33.1	14	38.9	14	41.2	13	27.7	203	37.2
	Unrestricted professional development funds	0	0.0	14	3.1	13	4.9	1	0.4	0	0.4	1	0.0	4	0.8	2	3.4	2	5.9	5	10.6	14	2.6
	Other (please specify)	43	43.9	116	25.9	90	33.8	69	24.6	52	24.6	32	28.4	39	24.6	9	33.6	12	35.3	15	31.9	159	29.1

Table continues p. 112

Table continued from p. 111

Item	Survey question	Two-year n	Two-year %	Four-year n	Four-year %	Public n	Public %	Private n	Private %	FY class size less than 500 n	FY class size less than 500 %	FY class size 501-1,000 n	FY class size 501-1,000 %	FY class size 1,001-2,000 n	FY class size 1,001-2,000 %	FY class size 2,001-3,000 n	FY class size 2,001-3,000 %	FY class size 3,001-4,000 n	FY class size 3,001-4,000 %	FY class size 4,001+ n	FY class size 4,001+ %	Total n	Total %
Q32	Type of compensation is offered to student affairs professionals for teaching the first-year seminar?																						
	No compensation is offered	39	36.8	109	33.7	91	37.3	57	30.8	45	34.1	36	36.4	27	32.9	17	38.6	11	32.4	12	31.6	148	34.5
	Graduate student support	0	0.0	2	0.6	2	0.8	0	0.0	0	0.0	0	0.0	0	0.0	1	2.3	1	2.9	0	0.0	2	0.5
	Release time	10	9.4	13	4.0	19	7.8	4	2.2	3	2.3	3	3.0	9	11.0	4	9.1	0	0.0	4	10.5	23	5.4
	Stipend	36	34.0	165	51.1	98	40.2	103	55.7	70	53.0	48	48.5	39	47.6	15	34.1	17	50.0	12	31.6	201	46.9
	Unrestricted professional development funds	1	0.9	7	2.2	7	2.9	1	0.5	1	0.8	3	3.0	0	0.0	1	2.3	0	0.0	3	7.9	8	1.9
	Other (please specify)	33	31.1	62	19.2	63	25.8	32	17.3	20	15.2	19	19.2	21	25.6	14	31.8	8	23.5	13	34.2	95	22.1
Q33	Type of compensation is offered to other campus professionals for teaching the first-year seminar?																						
	No compensation is offered	18	32.1	71	33.8	48	33.8	41	33.1	28	32.6	22	33.3	19	35.2	9	36.0	6	40.0	5	25.0	89	33.5
	Graduate student support	0	0.0	1	0.5	1	0.7	0	0.0	0	0.0	0	0.0	0	0.0	0	0.0	1	6.7	0	0.0	1	0.4
	Release time	3	5.4	8	3.8	8	5.6	3	2.4	3	3.5	1	1.5	4	7.4	2	8.0	0	0.0	1	5.0	11	4.1
	Stipend	16	28.6	102	48.6	58	40.8	60	48.4	43	50.0	25	37.9	23	42.6	14	56.0	6	40.0	7	35.0	118	44.4
	Unrestricted professional development funds	0	0.0	4	1.9	3	2.1	1	0.8	0	0.0	2	3.0	0	0.0	1	4.0	0	0.0	1	5.0	4	1.5
	Other (please specify)	26	46.4	50	23.8	49	34.5	27	21.8	18	20.9	18	27.3	21	38.9	7	28.0	4	26.7	8	40.0	76	28.6

Item	Survey question	Two-year n	Two-year %	Four-year n	Four-year %	Public n	Public %	Private n	Private %	FY class size less than 500 n	FY class size less than 500 %	FY class size 501-1,000 n	FY class size 501-1,000 %	FY class size 1,001-2,000 n	FY class size 1,001-2,000 %	FY class size 2,001-3,000 n	FY class size 2,001-3,000 %	FY class size 3,001-4,000 n	FY class size 3,001-4,000 %	FY class size 4,001+ n	FY class size 4,001+ %	Total n	Total %
Q34	Type of compensation is offered to graduate students for teaching the first-year seminar?																						
	No compensation is offered	1	100.0	17	34.7	15	40.5	3	23.1	0	0.0	2	22.2	4	28.6	6	66.7	3	50.0	3	37.5	18	36.0
	Stipend	0	0.0	27	55.1	17	45.9	10	76.9	4	100.0	6	66.7	7	50.0	3	33.3	4	66.7	3	37.5	27	54.0
	Other(please specify)	0	0.0	13	26.5	13	35.1	0	0.0	0	0.0	1	11.1	4	28.6	4	44.4	0	0.0	4	50.0	13	26.0
Q35	Amount of stipend per class for adjunct faculty:																						
	$500 or less	11	19.6	11	6.9	11	8.6	11	12.5	8	11.8	5	11.4	3	5.6	4	21.1	1	7.1	1	5.9	22	10.2
	$501 - $1,000	17	30.4	35	21.9	31	24.2	21	23.9	18	26.5	13	29.5	13	24.1	3	15.8	3	21.4	2	11.8	52	24.1
	$1,001 - $1,500	9	16.1	23	14.4	25	19.5	7	8.0	8	11.8	5	11.4	11	20.4	4	21.1	1	7.1	3	17.6	32	14.8
	$1,501 - $2,000	9	16.1	29	18.1	28	21.9	10	11.4	8	11.8	4	9.0	13	24.1	5	26.3	3	21.4	5	29.4	38	17.6
	$2,001 - $2,500	8	14.3	21	13.1	15	11.7	14	15.9	12	17.6	6	13.6	4	7.4	3	15.8	3	21.4	1	5.9	29	13.4
	$2,501 - $3,000	1	1.8	22	13.8	9	7.0	14	15.9	9	13.2	6	13.6	4	7.4	0	0.0	2	14.3	2	11.8	23	10.6
	$3,001 - $3,500	0	0.0	6	3.8	3	2.3	3	3.4	2	2.9	2	4.5	1	1.9	0	0.0	1	7.1	0	0.0	6	2.8
	$3,501 - $4,000	0	0.0	3	1.9	3	2.3	0	0.0	0	0.0	0	0.0	2	3.7	0	0.0	0	0.0	1	5.9	3	1.4
	$4,001 - $4,500	1	1.8	8	5.0	3	2.3	6	6.8	2	2.9	2	4.5	3	5.6	0	0.0	0	0.0	2	11.8	9	4.2
	$4,501 - $5,000	0	0.0	1	0.6	0	0.0	1	1.1	1	1.5	0	0.0	0	0.0	0	0.0	0	0.0	0	0.0	1	0.5
	More than $5,000	0	0.0	1	0.6	0	0.0	1	1.1	0	0.0	1	2.3	0	0.0	0	0.0	0	0.0	0	0.0	1	0.5
	Total	56	100.0	160	100.0	128	100.0	88	100.0	68	100.0	44	100.0	54	100.0	19	100.0	14	100.0	17	100.0	216	100.0

Table continues p. 114

Table continued from p. 113

Item	Survey question	Two-year		Four-year		Public		Private		FY class size less than 500		FY class size 501 - 1,000		FY class size 1,001 - 2,000		FY class size 2,001 - 3,000		FY class size 3,001 - 4,000		FY class size 4,001+		Total	
		n	%	n	%	n	%	n	%	n	%	n	%	n	%	n	%	n	%	n	%	n	%
Q36	Amount of stipend per class for tenure-track faculty:																						
	$500 or less	6	26.1	20	11.0	12	13.6	14	12.1	11	13.6	4	9.3	8	21.1	1	7.1	2	14.3	0	0.0	26	12.7
	$501 - $1,000	10	43.5	56	30.9	26	29.5	40	34.5	32	39.5	18	41.9	6	15.8	5	35.7	2	14.3	3	21.4	66	32.4
	$1,001 - $1,500	3	13.0	32	17.7	16	18.2	19	16.4	10	12.3	6	14.0	9	23.7	7	50.0	1	7.1	2	14.3	35	17.2
	$1,501 - $2,000	1	4.3	26	14.4	13	14.8	14	12.1	12	14.8	4	9.3	6	15.8	0	0.0	3	21.4	2	14.3	27	13.2
	$2,001 - $2,500	1	4.3	17	9.4	6	6.8	12	10.3	6	7.4	5	11.6	4	10.5	1	7.1	0	0.0	2	14.3	18	8.8
	$2,501 - $3,000	1	4.3	14	7.7	6	6.8	9	7.8	6	7.4	4	9.3	1	2.6	0	0.0	3	21.4	1	7.1	15	7.4
	$3,001 - $3,500	1	4.3	4	2.2	3	3.4	2	1.7	1	1.2	0	0.0	1	2.6	0	0.0	2	14.3	1	7.1	5	2.5
	$3,501 - $4,000	0	0.0	6	3.3	4	4.5	2	1.7	2	2.5	1	2.3	1	2.6	0	0.0	0	0.0	2	14.3	6	2.9
	$4,001 - $4,500	0	0.0	2	1.1	0	0.0	2	1.7	0	0.0	1	2.3	0	0.0	0	0.0	1	7.1	0	0.0	2	1.0
	$4,501 - $5,000	0	0.0	1	0.6	1	1.1	0	0.0	0	0.0	0	0.0	0	0.0	0	0.0	0	0.0	1	7.1	1	0.5
	More than $5,000	0	0.0	3	1.7	1	1.1	2	1.7	1	1.2	0	0.0	2	5.3	0	0.0	0	0.0	0	0.0	3	1.5
	Total	23	100.0	181	100.0	88	100.0	116	100.0	81	100.0	43	100.0	38	100.0	14	100.0	14	100.0	14	100.0	204	100.0
Q37	Amount of stipend per class for student affairs professionals:																						
	$500 or less	7	19.4	22	13.3	13	13.1	16	15.5	11	15.7	6	12.5	7	17.9	2	13.3	2	11.8	1	7.7	29	14.4
	$501 - $1,000	12	33.3	57	34.3	34	34.3	35	34.0	27	38.6	21	43.8	9	23.0	6	40.0	3	17.6	3	23.1	69	34.2
	$1,001 - $1,500	7	19.4	27	16.3	20	20.2	14	13.6	6	8.6	7	14.6	11	28.2	5	33.3	2	11.8	3	23.1	34	16.8
	$1,501 - $2,000	4	11.1	26	15.7	17	17.2	13	12.6	10	14.3	4	8.3	7	17.9	2	13.3	4	23.5	3	23.1	30	14.9
	$2,001 - $2,500	2	5.6	16	9.6	6	6.1	12	11.7	7	10.0	6	12.5	2	5.1	0	0.0	3	17.6	0	0.0	18	8.9
	$2,501 - $3,000	3	8.3	14	8.4	5	5.1	12	11.7	8	11.4	3	6.3	3	7.7	0	0.0	2	11.8	1	7.7	17	8.4

Item	Survey question	Two-year n	Two-year %	Four-year n	Four-year %	Public n	Public %	Private n	Private %	FY class size less than 500 n	FY class size less than 500 %	FY class size 501 - 1,000 n	FY class size 501 - 1,000 %	FY class size 1,001 - 2,000 n	FY class size 1,001 - 2,000 %	FY class size 2,001 - 3,000 n	FY class size 2,001 - 3,000 %	FY class size 3,001 - 4,000 n	FY class size 3,001 - 4,000 %	FY class size 4,001+ n	FY class size 4,001+ %	Total n	Total %
Q37	Amount of stipend per class for student affairs professionals: *(continued)*																						
	$3,001 - $3,500	1	2.8	2	1.2	2	2.0	1	1.0	1	1.4	0	0.0	0	0.0	0	0.0	1	5.9	1	7.7	3	1.5
	$3,501 - $4,000	0	0.0	1	0.6	1	1.0	0	0.0	0	0.0	1	2.1	0	0.0	0	0.0	0	0.0	0	0.0	1	0.5
	$4,001 - $4,500	0	0.0	1	0.6	1	1.0	0	0.0	0	0.0	0	0.0	0	0.0	0	0.0	0	0.0	1	7.7	1	0.5
	$4,501 - $5,000	0	0.0	0	0.0	0	0.0	0	0.0	0	0.0	0	0.0	0	0.0	0	0.0	0	0.0	0	0.0	0	0.0
	More than $5,000	0	0.0	0	0.0	0	0.0	0	0.0	0	0.0	0	0.0	0	0.0	0	0.0	0	0.0	0	0.0	0	0.0
	Total	36	100.0	166	100.0	99	100.0	103	100.0	70	100.0	48	100.0	39	100.0	15	100.0	17	100.0	13	100.0	202	100.0
Q38	Amount of stipend per class for other campus professionals:																						
	$500 or less	4	25.0	12	11.7	7	11.9	9	15.0	5	11.6	4	16.0	4	17.4	2	14.3	1	16.7	0	0.0	16	13.4
	$501 - $1,000	2	12.5	31	30.1	17	28.8	16	26.7	12	27.9	7	28.0	7	30.4	3	21.4	1	16.7	3	37.5	33	27.7
	$1,001 - $1,500	2	12.5	15	14.6	10	16.9	7	11.7	7	16.3	2	8.0	3	13.0	5	35.8	0	0.0	0	0.0	17	14.3
	$1,501 - $2,000	5	31.3	19	18.4	14	23.7	10	16.7	7	16.3	6	24.0	5	21.7	2	14.3	2	33.3	2	25.0	24	20.2
	$2,001 - $2,500	2	12.5	13	12.6	6	10.2	9	15.0	7	16.3	2	8.0	2	8.7	2	14.3	2	33.3	0	0.0	15	12.6
	$2,501 - $3,000	1	6.3	7	6.8	2	3.4	6	10.0	5	11.6	1	4.0	0	0.0	0	0.0	0	0.0	2	25.0	8	6.7
	$3,001 - $3,500	0	0.0	1	1.0	0	0.0	1	1.7	0	0.0	1	4.0	1	4.3	0	0.0	0	0.0	0	0.0	1	0.8
	$3,501 - $4,000	0	0.0	1	1.0	1	1.7	0	0.0	0	0.0	1	4.0	0	0.0	0	0.0	0	0.0	0	0.0	1	0.8
	$4,001 - $4,500	0	0.0	3	2.9	2	3.4	1	1.7	0	0.0	0	0.0	1	4.3	0	0.0	0	0.0	1	12.5	3	2.5
	$4,501 - $5,000	0	0.0	0	0.0	0	0.0	0	0.0	0	0.0	0	0.0	0	0.0	0	0.0	0	0.0	0	0.0	0	0.0
	More than $5,000	0	0.0	1	1.0	0	0.0	1	1.7	0	1.7	1	4.0	0	0.0	0	0.0	0	0.0	0	0.0	1	0.8
	Total	16	100.0	103	100.0	59	100.0	60	100.0	43	100.0	25	100.0	23	100.0	14	100.0	6	100.0	8	100.0	119	100.0

Table continues p. 116

Table continued from p. 115

Item	Survey question	Two-year n	Two-year %	Four-year n	Four-year %	Public n	Public %	Private n	Private %	FY class size less than 500 n	%	FY class size 501 - 1,000 n	%	FY class size 1,001 - 2,000 n	%	FY class size 2,001 - 3,000 n	%	FY class size 3,001 - 4,000 n	%	FY class size 4,001+ n	%	Total n	Total %
Q39	Amount of stipend per class for graduate students:																						
	$500 or less	0	0.0	10	37.3	2	11.8	8	72.7	2	50.0	4	66.7	3	42.9	0	0.0	1	25.0	0	0.0	10	37.0
	$501 - $1,000	0	0.0	6	22.2	5	29.4	1	9.1	1	25.0	1	16.7	2	28.6	1	33.3	1	25.0	0	0.0	6	22.2
	$1,001 - $1,500	0	0.0	6	22.2	6	35.3	1	9.1	1	25.0	1	16.7	1	14.3	1	33.3	1	25.0	1	33.3	6	22.2
	$1,501 - $2,000	0	0.0	2	7.4	2	11.8	0	0.0	0	0.0	0	0.0	0	0.0	0	0.0	1	25.0	1	33.3	2	7.4
	$2,001 - $2,500	0	0.0	1	3.7	1	5.9	0	0.0	0	0.0	0	0.0	0	0.0	1	33.3	0	0.0	0	0.0	1	3.7
	$2,501 - $3,000	0	0.0	0	0.0	0	0.0	0	0.0	0	0.0	0	0.0	0	0.0	0	0.0	0	0.0	0	0.0	0	0.0
	$3,001 - $3,500	0	0.0	0	0.0	0	0.0	0	0.0	0	0.0	0	0.0	0	0.0	0	0.0	0	0.0	0	0.0	0	0.0
	$3,501 - $4,000	0	0.0	0	0.0	0	0.0	0	0.0	0	0.0	0	0.0	0	0.0	0	0.0	0	0.0	0	0.0	0	0.0
	$4,001 - $4,500	0	0.0	1	3.7	0	0.0	1	9.1	0	0.0	0	0.0	1	14.3	0	0.0	0	0.0	0	0.0	1	3.7
	$4,501 - $5,000	0	0.0	0	0.0	0	0.0	0	0.0	0	0.0	0	0.0	0	0.0	0	0.0	0	0.0	0	0.0	0	0.0
	More than $5,000	0	0.0	1	3.7	1	5.9	0	0.0	0	0.0	0	0.0	0	0.0	0	0.0	0	0.0	1	33.3	1	3.7
	Total	0	100.0	27	100.0	17	100.0	11	100.0	4	100.0	6	100.0	7	100.0	3	100.0	4	100.0	3	100.0	27	100.0
Q43	Is instructor training offered for first-year seminar instructors?																						
	I don't know	12	5.5	14	2.2	18	4.1	8	1.9	6	2.0	7	3.5	5	3.0	1	1.4	2	3.9	5	7.8	26	3.1
	No	58	26.5	119	18.9	95	21.7	82	20.0	82	28.0	43	21.3	31	18.3	7	10.0	4	7.8	10	15.6	177	20.8
	Yes	149	68.0	497	78.9	325	74.2	321	78.1	205	70.0	152	75.2	133	78.7	62	88.6	45	88.2	49	76.6	646	76.1
	Total	219	100.0	630	100.0	438	100.0	411	100.0	293	100.0	202	100.0	169	100.0	70	100.0	51	100.0	64	100.0	849	100.0

Item	Survey question	Two-year		Four-year		Public		Private		FY class size less than 500		FY class size 501 - 1,000		FY class size 1,001 - 2,000		FY class size 2,001 - 3,000		FY class size 3,001 - 4,000		FY class size 4,001+		Total	
		n	%	n	%	n	%	n	%	n	%	n	%	n	%	n	%	n	%	n	%	n	%
Q44	Is instructor training required for first-year seminar instructors?																						
	I don't know	13	5.9	20	3.2	21	4.8	12	2.9	7	2.4	10	5.0	8	4.7	4	5.7	2	3.9	2	3.1	33	3.9
	No	112	51.1	279	44.3	210	47.9	181	44.0	149	50.9	87	43.1	78	46.2	23	32.9	29	49.0	29	45.3	391	46.1
	Yes	94	42.9	331	52.5	207	47.3	218	53.0	137	46.8	105	52.0	83	49.1	43	61.4	33	47.1	33	51.6	425	50.1
	Total	219	100.0	630	100.0	438	100.0	411	100.0	293	100.0	202	100.0	169	100.0	70	100.0	51	100.0	64	100.0	849	100.0
Q45	How long is new instructor training?																						
	Half a day or less	73	49.0	164	33.0	132	40.6	105	32.7	72	35.1	52	34.2	51	38.3	29	46.8	20	44.4	13	26.5	237	36.7
	1 day	32	21.5	108	21.7	68	20.9	72	22.4	43	21.0	41	27.0	27	20.3	10	16.1	10	22.2	9	18.4	140	21.7
	2 days	9	6.0	65	13.1	37	11.4	37	11.5	28	13.7	14	9.2	21	15.8	7	11.3	2	4.4	2	4.1	74	11.5
	3 days	9	6.0	24	4.8	15	4.6	18	5.6	12	5.9	8	5.3	8	6.0	3	4.8	2	4.4	0	0.0	33	5.1
	4 days	2	1.3	6	1.2	4	1.2	4	1.2	2	1.0	4	2.6	0	0.0	1	1.6	0	1.6	1	2.0	8	1.2
	1 week	4	2.7	16	3.2	7	2.2	13	4.0	9	4.4	3	2.0	3	2.3	0	0.0	2	4.4	3	6.1	20	3.1
	Other	20	13.4	114	22.9	62	19.1	72	22.4	39	19.0	30	19.7	23	17.3	12	19.4	9	20.0	21	42.9	134	20.7
	Total	149	100.0	497	100.0	325	100.0	321	100.0	205	100.0	152	100.0	133	100.0	62	100.0	45	100.0	49	100.0	646	100.0
Q46	Typical length of a section of the first-year seminar:																						
	Half a semester	40	18.3	67	10.7	56	12.8	51	12.4	36	12.4	33	16.4	19	11.2	9	12.9	5	9.8	5	7.8	107	12.6
	One quarter	17	7.8	33	5.2	28	6.4	22	5.4	18	6.1	12	6.0	8	4.7	5	7.1	4	7.8	3	4.7	50	5.9
	One semester	141	64.4	434	69.0	308	70.3	267	65.1	199	67.9	127	63.2	120	71.0	45	64.3	37	72.5	47	73.4	575	67.8
	One year	1	0.5	31	4.9	9	2.1	23	5.7	15	5.1	8	4.0	3	1.8	2	2.9	3	5.9	1	1.6	32	3.8
	Other	20	9.1	64	10.2	37	8.4	47	11.5	25	8.5	21	10.4	19	11.2	9	12.9	2	3.9	8	12.5	84	9.9
	Total	219	100.0	629	100.0	438	100.0	410	100.0	293	100.0	201	100.0	169	100.0	70	100.0	51	100.0	64	100.0	848	100.0

Table continues p. 118

Table continued from p. 117

Item	Survey question	Two-year		Four-year		Public		Private		FY class size less than 500		FY class size 501 - 1,000		FY class size 1,001 - 2,000		FY class size 2,001 - 3,000		FY class size 3,001 - 4,000		FY class size 4,001+		Total	
		n	%	n	%	n	%	n	%	n	%	n	%	n	%	n	%	n	%	n	%	n	%
Q47	**How is the first-year seminar graded?**																						
	Pass/fail	20	9.1	90	14.3	39	8.9	71	17.3	41	14.0	32	15.9	21	12.4	6	8.6	4	7.8	6	9.4	110	13.0
	Letter grade	186	84.9	497	79.0	372	84.9	311	75.6	236	80.5	156	77.6	139	82.2	60	85.7	41	80.4	51	79.7	683	80.5
	No grade	4	1.8	17	2.7	10	2.3	11	2.7	8	2.7	5	2.5	5	3.0	0	0.0	1	2.0	2	3.1	21	2.5
	Other	9	4.1	25	4.0	17	3.9	17	4.1	8	2.7	8	4.0	4	2.4	4	5.7	5	9.8	5	7.8	34	4.0
	Total	219	100.0	629	100.0	438	100.0	410	100.0	293	100.0	201	100.0	169	100.0	70	100.0	51	100.0	64	100.0	848	100.0
Q48	**Does the first-year seminar carry academic credit?**																						
	I don't know	0	0.0	2	0.3	1	0.2	1	0.2	0	0.0	0	0.0	0	0.0	0	0.0	2	3.9	0	0.0	2	0.2
	No	25	11.4	47	7.5	33	7.5	39	9.5	24	8.2	17	8.5	16	9.5	6	8.6	4	7.8	5	7.8	72	8.5
	Yes	194	88.6	580	92.2	404	92.2	370	90.2	269	91.8	184	91.5	153	90.5	64	91.4	45	88.2	59	92.2	774	91.3
	Total	219	100.0	629	100.0	438	100.0	410	100.0	293	100.0	201	100.0	169	100.0	70	100.0	51	100.0	64	100.0	848	100.0
Q49	**How many credits does the first-year seminar carry?**																						
	1	93	47.9	242	41.7	178	44.1	157	42.4	119	44.2	81	44.0	61	39.9	34	53.1	17	37.8	23	39.0	335	43.3
	2	27	13.9	82	14.1	68	16.8	41	11.1	34	12.6	28	15.2	23	15.0	9	14.1	6	13.3	9	15.3	109	14.1
	3	66	34.0	181	31.2	143	35.4	104	28.1	82	30.5	43	23.4	58	37.9	19	29.7	18	40.0	27	45.8	247	31.9
	4	3	1.5	62	10.7	6	1.5	59	15.9	32	11.9	24	13.0	7	4.6	1	1.6	1	1.6	0	0.0	65	8.4
	5	2	1.0	1	0.2	2	0.5	1	0.3	0	0.0	1	0.5	0	0.0	1	1.6	1	1.6	0	0.0	3	0.4
	More than 5	3	1.5	12	2.1	7	1.7	8	2.2	2	0.7	7	3.8	4	2.6	0	0.0	2	4.4	0	0.0	15	1.9
	Total	194	100.0	580	100.0	404	100.0	370	100.0	269	100.0	184	100.0	153	100.0	64	100.0	45	100.0	59	100.0	774	100.0

Item	Survey question	Two-year		Four-year		Public		Private		FY class size less than 500		FY class size 501 - 1,000		FY class size 1,001 - 2,000		FY class size 2,001 - 3,000		FY class size 3,001 - 4,000		FY class size 4,001+		Total	
		n	%	n	%	n	%	n	%	n	%	n	%	n	%	n	%	n	%	n	%	n	%
Q50	How is the first-year seminar credit applied? (Check all that apply)																						
	As an elective	116	59.8	192	33.1	238	58.9	70	18.9	54	20.1	70	38.0	76	49.7	37	57.8	28	62.2	43	72.9	308	39.8
	Toward general education requirements	64	33.0	347	59.8	145	35.9	266	71.9	189	70.3	97	52.7	69	45.1	21	32.8	17	37.8	18	30.5	411	53.1
	Toward major requirements	19	9.8	56	9.7	42	10.4	33	8.9	14	5.2	24	13.0	20	13.1	2	3.1	7	15.6	8	13.6	75	9.7
	Other (please specify)	16	8.2	57	9.8	39	9.7	34	9.2	21	7.8	21	11.4	13	8.5	9	14.1	4	8.9	5	8.5	73	9.4
Q51	Total classroom contact hours per week:																						
	1	54	24.7	172	27.3	106	24.2	120	29.3	87	29.7	47	23.4	41	24.3	20	28.6	17	33.3	14	21.9	226	26.7
	2	63	28.8	152	24.2	132	30.1	83	20.2	68	23.2	60	29.9	46	27.2	16	22.9	7	13.7	18	28.1	215	25.4
	3	88	40.2	241	38.3	181	41.3	148	36.1	105	35.8	66	32.8	73	43.2	29	41.4	25	49.0	31	48.4	329	38.8
	4	2	0.9	49	7.8	4	0.9	47	11.5	26	8.9	19	9.5	6	3.6	0	0.0	0	0.0	0	0.0	51	6.0
	More than 5	12	5.5	15	2.4	15	3.4	12	2.9	7	2.4	9	4.5	3	1.8	5	7.1	2	3.9	1	1.6	27	3.2
	Total	219	100.0	629	100.0	438	100.0	410	100.0	293	100.0	201	100.0	169	100.0	70	100.0	51	100.0	64	100.0	848	100.0
Q52	Do any sections include a service-learning component?																						
	I don't know	23	10.5	34	5.4	38	8.7	19	4.6	13	4.4	16	8.0	13	7.7	6	8.6	3	5.9	6	9.4	57	6.7
	No	153	69.9	296	47.1	226	51.6	223	54.4	156	53.2	112	55.7	91	53.8	39	55.7	24	47.1	27	42.2	449	52.9
	Yes	43	19.6	299	47.5	174	39.7	168	41.0	124	42.3	73	36.3	65	38.5	25	35.7	24	47.1	31	48.4	342	40.3
	Total	219	100.0	629	100.0	438	100.0	410	100.0	293	100.0	201	100.0	169	100.0	70	100.0	51	100.0	64	100.0	848	100.0

Table continues p. 120

Table continued from p. 119

Item	Survey question	Two-year n	Two-year %	Four-year n	Four-year %	Public n	Public %	Private n	Private %	FY class size less than 500 n	FY class size less than 500 %	FY class size 501-1,000 n	FY class size 501-1,000 %	FY class size 1,001-2,000 n	FY class size 1,001-2,000 %	FY class size 2,001-3,000 n	FY class size 2,001-3,000 %	FY class size 3,001-4,000 n	FY class size 3,001-4,000 %	FY class size 4,001+ n	FY class size 4,001+ %	Total n	Total %
Q54	Are any sections linked to one or more other courses?																						
	I don't know	7	3.2	6	1.0	9	2.1	4	1.0	2	0.7	5	2.5	4	2.4	1	1.4	1	2.0	0	0.0	13	1.5
	No	135	61.6	397	63.1	230	52.5	302	73.7	223	76.1	127	63.2	104	61.5	38	54.3	19	37.3	21	32.8	532	62.7
	Yes	77	35.2	226	35.9	199	45.4	104	25.4	68	23.2	69	34.3	61	36.1	31	44.3	31	60.8	43	67.2	303	35.7
	Total	219	100.0	629	100.0	438	100.0	410	100.0	293	100.0	201	100.0	169	100.0	70	100.0	51	100.0	64	100.0	848	100.0
Q55	Do any sections incorporate a first-year/summer reading program component?																						
	I don't know	6	2.7	6	1.0	10	2.3	2	0.5	2	0.7	4	2.0	4	2.4	0	0.0	0	0.0	2	3.1	12	1.4
	No	190	86.8	383	60.9	310	70.8	263	64.1	196	66.9	139	69.2	118	69.8	49	70.0	33	64.7	38	59.4	573	67.6
	Yes	23	10.5	240	38.2	118	26.9	145	35.4	95	32.4	58	28.9	47	27.8	21	30.0	18	35.3	24	37.5	263	31.0
	Total	219	100.0	629	100.0	438	100.0	410	100.0	293	100.0	201	100.0	169	100.0	70	100.0	51	100.0	64	100.0	848	100.0
Q57	Do any sections incorporate online components?																						
	I don't know	17	7.8	54	8.6	38	8.7	33	8.1	19	6.5	20	10.0	15	8.9	1	1.4	6	11.8	10	15.6	71	8.4
	No	67	30.6	261	41.6	127	29.0	201	49.1	143	48.8	84	42.0	56	33.1	18	25.7	10	19.6	17	26.6	328	38.7
	Yes	135	61.6	313	49.8	273	62.3	175	42.8	131	44.7	96	48.0	98	58.0	51	72.9	35	68.6	37	57.8	448	52.9
	Total	219	100.0	628	100.0	438	100.0	409	100.0	293	100.0	200	100.0	169	100.0	70	100.0	51	100.0	64	100.0	847	100.0
Q59	Are there any online-only sections?																						
	I don't know	7	3.2	2	0.3	7	1.6	2	0.5	2	0.7	1	0.5	1	0.6	0	0.0	2	3.9	3	4.7	9	1.1
	No	140	63.9	575	91.6	335	76.5	380	92.9	269	91.8	178	89.0	137	81.1	45	64.3	40	78.4	46	71.9	715	84.4
	Yes	72	32.9	51	8.1	96	21.9	27	6.6	22	7.5	21	10.5	31	18.3	25	35.7	9	17.6	15	23.4	123	14.5
	Total	219	100.0	628	100.0	438	100.0	409	100.0	293	100.0	200	100.0	169	100.0	70	100.0	51	100.0	64	100.0	847	100.0

Item	Survey question	Two-year		Four-year		Public		Private		FY class size less than 500		FY class size 501 - 1,000		FY class size 1,001 - 2,000		FY class size 2,001 - 3,000		FY class size 3,001 - 4,000		FY class size 4,001+		Total	
		n	%	n	%	n	%	n	%	n	%	n	%	n	%	n	%	n	%	n	%	n	%
Q60	Approximate percentage of online-only sections:																						
	Less than 10%	38	52.8	31	60.8	57	59.4	12	44.4	11	50.0	13	61.9	17	54.8	14	56.0	5	55.6	9	60.0	69	56.1
	10% - 19%	11	15.3	5	9.8	14	14.6	2	7.4	3	13.6	3	14.3	3	9.7	5	20.0	1	11.1	1	6.7	16	13.0
	20% - 29%	12	16.7	3	5.9	12	12.5	3	11.1	5	22.7	0	0.0	6	19.4	1	4.0	1	11.1	2	13.3	15	12.2
	30% - 39%	5	6.9	1	2.0	6	6.3	0	0.0	0	0.0	1	4.8	3	9.7	1	4.0	1	11.1	0	0.0	6	4.9
	40% - 49%	3	4.2	0	0.0	3	3.1	0	0.0	0	0.0	1	4.8	1	3.2	1	4.0	0	0.0	0	0.0	3	2.4
	50% - 59%	2	2.8	2	3.9	2	2.1	2	7.4	2	9.1	0	0.0	1	3.2	0	0.0	0	0.0	1	6.7	4	3.3
	60% - 69%	0	0.0	1	2.0	0	0.0	1	3.7	0	0.0	0	0.0	0	0.0	1	4.0	0	0.0	0	0.0	1	0.8
	70% - 79%	0	0.0	0	0.0	0	0.0	0	0.0	0	0.0	0	0.0	0	0.0	0	0.0	0	0.0	0	0.0	0	0.0
	80% - 89%	0	0.0	1	2.0	1	1.0	0	0.0	1	4.5	0	0.0	0	0.0	0	0.0	0	0.0	0	0.0	1	0.8
	90% - 99%	0	0.0	0	0.0	0	0.0	0	0.0	0	0.0	0	0.0	0	0.0	0	0.0	0	0.0	0	0.0	0	0.0
	100%	1	1.4	7	13.7	1	1.0	7	25.9	0	0.0	3	14.3	0	0.0	2	8.0	1	11.1	2	13.3	8	6.5
	Total	72	100.0	51	100.0	96	100.0	27	100.0	22	100.0	21	100.0	31	100.0	25	100.0	9	100.0	15	100.0	123	100.0
Q61	Campus unit directly administers the first-year seminar?																						
	Academic affairs	66	30.1	247	39.3	135	31.0	178	43.5	132	45.1	85	42.5	48	28.4	20	28.6	14	27.5	14	21.9	313	37.0
	Academic department(s)	72	32.9	66	10.5	91	20.8	47	11.5	40	13.7	22	11.0	32	18.9	14	20.0	13	25.5	17	26.6	138	16.3
	College or school	11	5.0	56	8.9	38	8.7	29	7.1	17	5.8	17	8.5	18	10.7	3	4.3	4	7.8	8	12.5	67	7.9
	First-year program office	8	3.7	93	14.8	48	11.0	53	13.0	27	9.2	29	14.5	23	13.6	11	15.7	6	11.8	5	7.8	101	11.9
	Student affairs	38	17.4	80	12.7	57	13.0	61	14.9	46	15.7	28	14.0	23	13.6	10	14.3	8	15.7	3	4.7	118	13.9
	Other	24	11.0	86	13.7	69	15.8	41	10.0	31	10.6	19	9.5	25	14.8	12	17.1	6	11.8	17	26.6	110	13.0
	Total	219	100.0	628	100.0	438	100.0	409	100.0	293	100.0	200	100.0	169	100.0	70	100.0	51	100.0	64	100.0	847	100.0

Table continues p. 122

Table continued from p. 121

Item	Survey question	Two-year n	Two-year %	Four-year n	Four-year %	Public n	Public %	Private n	Private %	FY class size less than 500 n	%	FY class size 501–1,000 n	%	FY class size 1,001–2,000 n	%	FY class size 2,001–3,000 n	%	FY class size 3,001–4,000 n	%	FY class size 4,001+ n	%	Total n	Total %
Q62	Is there a dean/director/coordinator of the first-year seminar?																						
	I don't know	3	1.4	1	0.2	3	0.7	1	0.2	1	0.3	1	0.5	0	0.0	1	1.4	0	0.0	1	1.7	4	0.5
	No	76	34.7	131	20.9	126	28.8	81	19.8	69	23.5	53	26.5	37	21.9	13	18.6	16	31.4	19	29.7	207	24.4
	Yes	140	63.9	496	79.0	309	70.5	327	80.0	223	76.1	146	73.0	132	78.1	56	80.0	35	68.6	44	68.8	636	75.1
	Total	219	100.0	628	100.0	438	100.0	409	100.0	293	100.0	200	100.0	169	100.0	70	100.0	51	100.0	64	100.0	847	100.0
Q63	Does the dean/director/coordinator of the first-year seminar work full time or less than full time in this position?																						
	Less than full time	84	60.0	312	62.9	179	57.9	217	66.4	164	73.5	91	62.3	73	55.3	26	46.4	16	45.7	26	59.1	396	62.3
	Full time (approximately 40 hr/wk)	56	40.0	184	37.1	130	42.1	110	33.4	59	26.5	55	37.7	59	44.7	30	53.6	19	54.3	18	40.9	240	37.7
	Total	140	100.0	496	100.0	309	100.0	327	100.0	223	100.0	146	100.0	132	100.0	56	100.0	35	100.0	44	100.0	636	100.0
Q64	Does the dean/director/coordinator have another position on campus?																						
	I don't know	0	0.0	0	0.0	0	0.0	0	0.0	0	0.0	0	0.0	0	0.0	0	0.0	0	0.0	0	0.0	0	0.0
	No	3	3.6	6	1.9	4	2.3	5	2.3	3	1.8	2	2.2	0	0.0	2	7.7	1	6.7	1	3.8	9	2.3
	Yes	81	96.4	304	98.1	173	97.7	212	97.7	161	98.2	89	97.8	72	100.0	24	92.3	14	93.3	25	96.2	385	97.7
	Total	84	100.0	310	100.0	177	100.0	217	100.0	164	100.0	91	100.0	72	100.0	26	100.0	15	100.0	26	100.0	394	100.0
Q65	The dean/director/coordinator's other campus role is as a/an:																						
	Academic affairs administrator	19	23.5	91	29.9	53	30.6	57	26.9	40	24.8	29	32.6	20	27.8	6	25.0	5	35.7	10	40.0	110	28.6
	Faculty member	18	22.2	98	32.2	51	29.5	65	30.7	42	26.1	33	37.1	20	27.8	6	25.0	5	35.7	10	40.0	116	30.1

Item	Survey question	Two-year		Four-year		Public		Private		FY class size less than 500		FY class size 501 - 1,000		FY class size 1,001 - 2,000		FY class size 2,001 - 3,000		FY class size 3,001 - 4,000		FY class size 4,001+		Total	
		n	%	n	%	n	%	n	%	n	%	n	%	n	%	n	%	n	%	n	%	n	%
Q65	The dean/director/coordinator's other campus role is as a/an: *(continued)*																						
	Student affairs administrator	19	23.5	89	29.3	50	28.9	58	27.4	38	23.6	28	31.5	21	29.2	6	25.0	5	35.7	10	40.0	108	28.1
	Other (please specify)	18	22.2	88	28.9	51	29.5	55	25.9	37	23.0	28	31.5	20	27.8	6	25.0	5	35.7	10	40.0	106	27.5
Q66	Select the three most important course objectives for the first-year seminar:																						
	Create common first-year experience	35	14.9	172	26.3	81	17.5	126	29.6	83	27.2	54	25.7	36	20.3	11	14.9	13	24.1	10	14.3	207	23.3
	Develop a connection with the institution	121	51.5	326	49.8	241	51.9	206	48.4	156	51.2	93	44.3	94	53.1	41	55.4	26	48.2	37	52.9	447	50.2
	Develop academic skills	134	57.0	352	53.7	270	58.2	216	50.7	159	52.1	109	51.9	102	57.6	47	63.5	36	66.7	33	47.1	486	54.6
	Develop financial literacy	7	3.0	3	0.5	9	1.9	1	0.2	3	1.0	0	0.0	6	3.4	0	0.0	0	0.0	1	1.4	10	1.1
	Develop support network/friendships	35	14.9	120	18.3	76	16.4	79	18.5	65	21.3	40	19.1	21	11.9	8	10.8	6	11.1	15	21.4	155	17.4
	Develop writing skills	15	6.4	91	13.9	27	5.8	79	18.5	44	14.4	32	15.2	20	15.2	5	11.3	3	6.8	2	5.6	106	11.9
	Improve sophomore return rates	28	11.9	110	16.8	77	16.6	61	14.3	55	18.0	32	15.2	19	10.7	12	16.2	12	22.2	8	11.4	138	15.5

Table continues p. 124

Table continued from p. 123

Item	Survey question	Two-year		Four-year		Public		Private		FY class size less than 500		FY class size 501 - 1,000		FY class size 1,001 - 2,000		FY class size 2,001 - 3,000		FY class size 3,001 - 4,000		FY class size 4,001+		Total	
		n	%	n	%	n	%	n	%	n	%	n	%	n	%	n	%	n	%	n	%	n	%
Q66	Select the three most important course objectives for the first-year seminar: *(continued)*																						
	Increase student/faculty interaction	14	6.0	136	20.8	60	12.9	90	21.1	48	15.7	41	19.5	28	15.8	11	14.9	9	16.7	13	18.6	150	16.9
	Introduce a discipline	5	2.1	57	8.7	31	6.7	31	7.3	14	4.6	16	7.6	17	9.6	3	4.1	6	11.1	6	8.6	62	7.0
	Provide orientation to campus resources and services	156	66.4	268	40.9	259	55.8	165	38.7	130	42.6	94	44.8	102	57.6	37	50.0	25	46.3	36	51.4	424	47.6
	Self-exploration/personal development	87	37.0	167	25.5	135	29.1	119	27.9	93	30.5	58	27.6	44	24.9	24	32.4	13	24.1	22	31.4	254	28.5
	Encourage arts participation	1	0.4	4	0.6	2	0.4	3	0.7	3	1.0	2	1.0	0	0.0	0	0.0	0	0.0	0	0.0	5	0.6
	Other (please specify)	13	5.5	59	9.0	31	6.7	41	9.6	22	9.6	20	7.2	10	9.5	9	5.7	4	12.2	7	7.4	72	8.1
Q67	The three most important topics that compose the content of this first-year seminar:																						
	Academic planning/advising	102	43.4	216	33.0	185	39.9	133	31.2	106	34.8	73	34.8	61	34.5	31	34.5	23	41.9	24	42.6	318	34.3
	Career exploration/preparation	43	18.3	95	14.5	84	18.1	54	12.7	41	13.4	37	17.6	28	15.8	14	15.8	9	18.9	9	16.7	138	12.9
	Campus resources	132	56.2	245	37.4	240	51.7	137	32.2	108	32.2	90	35.4	76	42.9	42	42.9	27	56.8	34	50.0	377	48.6

Item	Survey question	Two-year		Four-year		Public		Private		FY class size less than 500		FY class size 501 - 1,000		FY class size 1,001 - 2,000		FY class size 2,001 - 3,000		FY class size 3,001 - 4,000		FY class size 4,001+		Total	
		n	%	n	%	n	%	n	%	n	%	n	%	n	%	n	%	n	%	n	%	n	%
Q67	The three most important topics that compose the content of this first-year seminar: *(continued)*																						
	College policies and procedures	42	17.9	92	14.1	66	14.2	68	16.0	47	15.4	29	13.8	34	19.2	9	12.2	5	9.3	10	14.3	134	15.1
	Critical thinking	44	18.7	266	40.6	126	27.2	184	43.2	122	40.0	79	37.6	54	30.5	22	29.7	15	27.8	18	25.7	310	34.8
	Diversity issues	3	1.3	58	8.9	27	5.8	34	8.0	24	7.9	15	7.1	9	5.1	3	4.1	2	3.7	8	11.4	61	6.9
	Financial literacy	3	1.3	6	0.9	7	1.5	2	0.5	1	0.3	4	1.9	4	2.3	0	0.0	0	0.0	0	0.0	9	1.0
	Health and wellness	6	2.6	27	4.1	14	3.0	19	4.5	13	4.3	6	2.9	9	5.1	1	1.4	3	5.6	1	1.4	33	3.7
	Relationship issues	17	7.2	65	9.9	25	5.4	57	13.4	44	14.4	18	8.6	9	5.1	4	5.4	5	9.3	2	2.9	82	9.2
	Specific disciplinary topic	4	1.7	121	18.5	46	9.9	79	18.5	43	14.1	40	19.1	23	13.0	2	2.7	7	13.0	10	14.3	125	14.0
	Study skills	140	59.6	214	32.7	224	48.3	130	30.5	118	38.7	69	32.9	74	41.8	36	48.7	28	51.9	29	41.4	354	39.8
	Time management	81	34.5	165	25.2	146	31.5	100	23.5	79	25.9	52	24.8	51	28.8	25	33.8	17	31.5	22	31.4	246	27.6
	Writing skills	13	5.5	141	21.5	39	8.4	115	27.0	72	23.6	40	19.1	24	13.6	7	9.5	5	9.3	6	8.6	154	17.3
	Other (please specify)	18	7.7	114	17.4	51	11.0	81	19.0	48	15.7	32	15.2	26	14.7	11	14.9	6	11.1	9	12.9	132	14.8
Q70	Has your first-year seminar been formally assessed or evaluated since fall 2006?																						
	I don't know	31	14.2	51	8.2	45	10.4	37	9.1	21	7.2	24	12.2	17	10.2	7	10.0	5	9.8	8	12.5	82	9.8
	No	97	44.5	187	30.0	167	38.5	117	28.7	96	32.9	70	35.5	60	35.9	24	34.3	18	35.3	16	25.0	284	33.8
	Yes	90	41.3	385	61.8	222	51.2	253	62.2	175	60.0	103	52.3	90	53.9	39	55.7	28	54.9	40	62.5	475	56.5
	Total	218	100.0	623	100.0	434	100.0	407	100.0	292	100.0	197	100.0	167	100.0	70	100.0	51	100.0	64	100.0	841	100.0

Table continues p. 126

Table continued from p. 125

Item	Survey question	Two-year n	Two-year %	Four-year n	Four-year %	Public n	Public %	Private n	Private %	FY class size less than 500 n	%	FY class size 501-1,000 n	%	FY class size 1,001-2,000 n	%	FY class size 2,001-3,000 n	%	FY class size 3,001-4,000 n	%	FY class size 4,001+ n	%	Total n	Total %
Q71	Analysis of institutional data (e.g., GPA, retention rates, graduation)																						
	I don't know	2	2.2	18	4.7	6	2.7	14	5.5	11	6.3	5	4.9	2	2.2	0	0.0	1	3.6	1	2.5	20	4.2
	No	17	18.8	80	20.8	35	15.8	62	24.5	42	24.1	22	21.4	19	21.1	6	15.4	6	21.4	2	5.0	97	20.5
	Yes	71	78.9	286	74.5	180	81.4	177	70.0	121	69.5	76	73.8	69	76.7	33	84.6	21	75.0	37	92.5	357	75.3
	Total	90	100.0	384	100.0	221	100.0	253	100.0	174	100.0	103	100.0	90	100.0	39	100.0	28	100.0	40	100.0	474	100.0
Q72	Focus groups with instructors																						
	I don't know	4	4.4	20	5.2	16	7.2	8	3.2	9	5.2	5	4.9	3	3.3	4	10.3	1	3.6	2	5.0	24	5.1
	No	48	53.3	159	41.4	107	48.4	100	39.5	78	44.8	39	37.9	43	47.8	14	35.9	13	46.4	20	50.0	207	43.7
	Yes	38	42.2	205	53.3	98	44.3	145	57.3	87	50.0	59	57.3	44	48.9	21	53.8	14	50.0	18	45.0	243	51.3
	Total	90	100.0	384	100.0	221	100.0	253	100.0	174	100.0	103	100.0	90	100.0	39	100.0	28	100.0	40	100.0	474	100.0
Q73	Focus groups with students																						
	I don't know	2	2.2	24	6.3	12	5.4	14	5.5	13	7.5	7	6.8	3	3.3	2	5.1	1	3.6	0	0.0	26	5.5
	No	55	61.1	191	49.7	118	53.4	128	50.6	88	50.6	58	56.3	46	51.1	18	46.2	16	46.4	20	50.0	246	51.9
	Yes	33	36.7	169	44.0	91	41.2	111	43.9	73	42.0	38	36.9	41	45.6	19	48.7	11	50.0	20	50.0	202	42.6
	Total	90	100.0	384	100.0	221	100.0	253	100.0	174	100.0	103	100.0	90	100.0	39	100.0	28	100.0	40	100.0	474	100.0
Q74	Individual interviews with instructors																						
	I don't know	9	10.0	24	6.3	18	8.1	15	5.9	12	6.9	9	8.7	2	2.2	2	5.1	4	14.3	4	10.0	33	7.0
	No	41	45.6	184	47.9	98	44.3	127	50.2	89	51.2	46	44.7	43	47.8	19	48.7	10	35.7	18	45.0	225	47.5
	Yes	40	44.4	176	45.8	105	47.5	111	43.9	73	42.0	48	46.6	45	46.6	18	50.0	14	46.2	18	45.0	216	45.6
	Total	90	100.0	384	100.0	221	100.0	253	100.0	174	100.0	103	100.0	90	100.0	39	100.0	28	100.0	40	100.0	474	100.0

Item	Survey question	Two-year n	Two-year %	Four-year n	Four-year %	Public n	Public %	Private n	Private %	FY class size less than 500 n	%	FY class size 501-1,000 n	%	FY class size 1,001-2,000 n	%	FY class size 2,001-3,000 n	%	FY class size 3,001-4,000 n	%	FY class size 4,001+ n	%	Total n	Total %
Q75	Individual interviews with students																						
	I don't know	8	8.9	28	7.3	19	8.6	17	6.7	16	9.2	7	6.8	3	3.3	4	10.3	4	14.3	2	5.0	36	7.6
	No	56	62.2	239	62.2	138	62.4	157	62.1	107	61.5	63	61.2	56	62.2	26	66.7	17	60.7	26	65.0	295	62.2
	Yes	26	28.9	117	30.5	64	29.0	79	31.2	51	29.3	33	32.0	31	34.4	9	23.1	7	25.0	12	30.0	143	30.2
	Total	90	100.0	384	100.0	221	100.0	253	100.0	174	100.0	103	100.0	90	100.0	39	100.0	28	100.0	40	100.0	474	100.0
Q76	Student course evaluation																						
	I don't know	3	3.3	2	0.8	3	1.4	2	0.8	3	1.7	1	1.0	1	1.1	0	0.0	0	0.0	0	0.0	5	1.1
	No	5	5.6	14	3.6	6	2.7	13	5.1	6	3.4	4	3.9	4	4.4	2	5.1	2	7.1	1	2.5	19	4.0
	Yes	82	91.1	368	95.8	212	95.9	238	94.1	165	94.8	98	95.1	85	94.4	37	94.9	26	92.9	39	97.5	450	94.9
	Total	90	100.0	384	100.0	221	100.0	253	100.0	174	100.0	103	100.0	90	100.0	39	100.0	28	100.0	40	100.0	474	100.0
Q77	Survey instrument																						
	I don't know	5	5.6	15	3.9	12	5.4	8	3.2	10	5.7	1	1.0	1	1.1	3	7.7	4	14.3	1	2.5	20	4.2
	No	20	22.2	77	20.1	46	20.8	51	20.2	39	22.4	19	18.4	19	21.1	9	23.1	4	14.3	7	17.5	97	20.5
	Yes	65	72.2	292	76.0	163	73.8	194	76.7	125	71.8	83	80.6	70	77.8	27	69.2	20	71.4	32	80.0	357	75.3
	Total	90	100.0	384	100.0	221	100.0	253	100.0	174	100.0	103	100.0	90	100.0	39	100.0	28	100.0	40	100.0	474	100.0
Q78	Type of survey instrument institution used to assess the first-year seminar? (Check all that apply)																						
	I don't know	3	4.6	6	2.1	5	3.1	4	2.1	3	2.4	2	2.4	3	4.3	0	0.0	0	0.0	1	3.1	9	2.5
	A locally developed	54	83.1	246	84.2	136	83.4	164	84.5	107	85.6	72	86.7	55	78.6	23	85.2	17	85.0	26	81.3	300	84.0
	A national survey (e.g., NSSE, CCSSE, CIRP, EBI)	25	38.5	162	55.5	81	49.7	106	54.6	71	56.8	36	43.4	37	52.9	13	48.1	11	55.0	19	59.4	187	52.4

Table continues p. 128

Table continued from p. 127

Item	Survey question	Two-year n	Two-year %	Four-year n	Four-year %	Public n	Public %	Private n	Private %	FY class size less than 500 n	FY class size less than 500 %	FY class size 501-1,000 n	FY class size 501-1,000 %	FY class size 1,001-2,000 n	FY class size 1,001-2,000 %	FY class size 2,001-3,000 n	FY class size 2,001-3,000 %	FY class size 3,001-4,000 n	FY class size 3,001-4,000 %	FY class size 4,001+ n	FY class size 4,001+ %	Total n	Total %
Q79	National survey was used: (Check all that apply)																						
	Community College Survey of Student Engagement (CCSSE)	24	96.0	0	0.0	24	29.6	0	0.0	2	2.8	4	11.1	4	10.8	5	38.5	2	18.2	7	36.8	24	12.8
	Cooperative Institutional Research Program (CIRP) Freshman Survey	0	0.0	66	40.7	18	22.2	48	45.3	33	46.5	10	27.8	12	32.4	3	23.1	4	36.4	4	21.1	66	35.3
	Cooperative Institutional Research Program (CIRP) Your First College Year (YFCY)	0	0.0	22	13.6	7	8.6	15	14.2	7	9.9	5	13.9	7	18.9	2	15.4	1	9.1	0	0.0	22	11.8
	First-Year Initiative (FYI)	1	4.0	17	10.5	10	12.3	8	7.5	3	4.2	2	5.6	8	21.6	3	23.1	2	18.2	0	0.0	18	9.6
	National Survey of Student Engagement (NSSE)	3	12.0	135	83.3	55	67.9	83	78.3	55	77.5	30	83.3	25	67.6	9	69.2	8	72.7	11	57.9	138	73.8
	Other (please specify)	5	20.0	34	21.0	15	18.5	24	22.6	12	16.9	11	30.6	9	24.3	0	0.0	3	27.3	4	21.1	39	20.9

Item	Survey question	Two-year		Four-year		Public		Private		FY class size less than 500		FY class size 501 - 1,000		FY class size 1,001 - 2,000		FY class size 2,001 - 3,000		FY class size 3,001 - 4,000		FY class size 4,001+		Total	
		n	%	n	%	n	%	n	%	n	%	n	%	n	%	n	%	n	%	n	%	n	%
Q81	Each outcome that was measured: (Check all that apply)																						
	Academic abilities	29	40.8	121	42.3	78	43.3	72	40.7	52	43.0	24	31.6	31	44.9	15	45.5	11	52.4	17	45.9	150	42.0
	Connections with peers	22	31.0	154	53.8	78	43.3	98	55.4	65	53.7	35	46.1	37	53.6	14	42.4	7	33.3	18	48.6	176	49.3
	Grade point average	42	59.2	165	57.7	120	66.7	87	49.2	62	51.2	40	52.6	41	59.4	24	72.7	15	71.4	25	67.6	207	58.0
	Out-of-class student/faculty interaction	21	29.6	147	51.4	81	45.0	87	49.2	60	49.6	34	44.7	34	49.3	15	45.5	9	42.9	16	43.2	168	47.1
	Participation in campus activities	25	35.2	150	52.4	89	49.4	86	48.6	58	47.9	37	48.7	37	53.6	17	51.5	12	57.1	14	37.8	175	49.0
	Persistence to graduation	26	36.6	111	38.8	80	44.4	57	32.2	42	34.7	24	31.6	28	40.6	16	48.5	9	42.9	18	48.6	137	38.4
	Persistence to sophomore year	41	57.7	222	77.6	144	80.0	119	67.2	83	68.6	52	68.4	54	78.3	26	78.8	18	85.7	30	81.1	263	73.7
	Satisfaction with faculty	38	53.5	215	75.2	122	67.8	131	74.0	90	74.4	55	72.4	47	68.1	20	60.6	14	66.7	27	73.0	253	70.9
	Satisfaction with the institution	34	47.9	199	69.6	102	56.7	131	74.0	91	75.2	54	71.1	37	53.6	18	54.5	9	54.5	24	64.9	233	65.3
	Use of campus services	30	42.3	152	53.1	93	51.7	89	50.3	58	47.9	38	50.0	34	49.3	18	54.5	12	57.1	22	59.5	182	51.0
	Other (please specify)	17	23.9	49	17.1	37	20.6	29	16.4	19	15.7	12	15.8	13	18.8	9	27.3	6	28.6	7	18.9	66	18.5

Table continued from p. 129

Item	Survey question	Two-year		Four-year		Public		Private		FY class size less than 500		FY class size 501 - 1,000		FY class size 1,001 - 2,000		FY class size 2,001 - 3,000		FY class size 3,001 - 4,000		FY class size 4,001+		Total	
		n	%	n	%	n	%	n	%	n	%	n	%	n	%	n	%	n	%	n	%	n	%
Q83	Release of data:																						
	Please do not share my survey responses	89	41.0	253	40.9	171	39.9	171	42.1	126	43.3	72	36.7	68	41.2	25	35.7	22	43.1	29	46.8	342	41.0
	You may share my survey responses	128	58.9	365	59.1	258	60.1	235	57.9	165	56.7	124	63.3	97	58.8	45	64.3	29	56.9	33	53.2	493	59.0
	Total	217	100.0	618	100.0	429	100.0	406	100.0	291	100.0	196	100.0	165	100.0	70	100.0	51	100.0	62	100.0	835	100.0

Percentages may not sum to 100.0% due to rounding.

All Responses by Seminar Type

Item	Survey question	Extended orientation seminar		Academic seminar: uniform content		Academic seminar: various topics		Preprofessional or discipline-linked seminar		Basic study skills seminar		Hybrid		Total	
		n	%	n	%	n	%	n	%	n	%	n	%	n	%
Q10	Percentage of first-year students who take a first-year seminar course														
	Less than 10%	22	6.2	9	6.5	4	3.0	2	6.3	13	31.0	8	6.1	67	7.6
	10% - 19%	28	7.9	7	5.0	11	8.3	3	9.4	7	16.7	2	1.5	59	6.7
	20% - 29%	28	7.9	8	5.8	6	4.5	4	12.5	5	11.9	6	4.6	60	6.8
	30% - 39%	28	7.9	5	3.6	7	5.3	3	9.4	1	2.4	8	6.1	54	6.1
	40% - 49%	7	2.0	3	2.2	4	3.0	0	0.0	1	2.4	3	2.3	21	2.4
	50% - 59%	16	4.5	2	1.4	5	3.8	2	6.3	1	2.4	5	3.8	32	3.6
	60% - 69%	15	4.2	3	2.2	1	0.8	2	6.3	0	0.0	3	2.3	25	2.8
	70% - 79%	22	6.2	3	2.2	5	3.8	2	6.3	3	7.1	5	3.8	43	4.9
	80% - 89%	34	9.6	9	6.5	4	3.0	4	12.5	3	7.1	11	8.3	66	7.5
	90% - 99%	73	20.6	40	28.8	18	13.5	6	18.8	4	9.5	34	25.8	182	20.7
	100%	81	22.9	50	36.0	68	51.1	4	12.5	4	9.5	47	35.6	270	30.7
	Total	354	100.0	139	100.0	133	100.0	32	100.0	42	100.0	132	100.0	879	100.0
Q11	Years a first-year seminar offered on campus?														
	Two years or less	51	14.4	17	12.2	13	9.8	6	18.8	9	21.4	14	10.6	121	13.8
	Three to 10 years	150	42.4	70	50.4	49	36.8	17	53.1	18	42.9	55	41.7	378	43.0
	More than 10 years	153	43.2	52	37.4	71	53.4	9	28.1	15	35.7	63	47.7	380	43.2
	Total	354	100.0	139	100.0	133	100.0	32	100.0	42	100.0	132	100.0	879	100.0

Table continues p. 132

Table continued from p. 131

Item	Survey question	Extended orientation seminar		Academic seminar: uniform content		Academic seminar: various topics		Preprofessional or discipline-linked seminar		Basic study skills seminar		Hybrid		Total	
		n	%	n	%	n	%	n	%	n	%	n	%	n	%
Q12	Select each discrete type of first-year seminar that exist on your campus: (Check all that apply)														
	Extended orientation seminar	350	98.9	59	42.5	28	21.1	16	50.0	26	61.9	47	35.6	549	61.7
	Academic seminar with uniform academic content	46	13.0	123	88.5	16	12.0	10	31.3	9	21.4	19	14.4	230	25.8
	Academic seminar on various topics	30	8.5	16	11.5	122	91.7	6	18.8	8	19.1	16	12.1	208	23.4
	Preprofessional or discipline-linked seminar	48	13.6	20	14.4	17	12.8	27	84.4	1	2.4	10	7.6	128	14.4
	Basic study skills seminar	79	22.3	36	25.9	13	9.8	6	18.8	38	90.5	18	13.6	199	22.4
	Hybrid	26	7.3	12	8.6	11	8.3	9	28.1	10	23.8	122	92.4	4	1.1
	Other	4	1.1	3	2.2	4	3.0	0	0.0	1	2.4	2	1.5	22	2.5
Q16	Approximate number of sections seminar type will be offered in the 2009/2010 academic year:														
	0	0	0.0	0	0.0	0	0.0	0	0.0	0	0.0	0	0.0	0	0.0
	1 - 10	82	23.2	41	29.5	17	12.8	12	37.5	20	47.6	32	24.2	217	25.2
	11 - 20	89	25.1	43	30.9	37	27.8	11	34.4	12	28.6	42	31.8	242	28.1
	21 - 30	60	17.0	27	19.4	24	18.1	3	9.4	4	9.5	24	18.2	145	16.8
	31 - 40	30	8.5	5	3.6	19	14.3	1	3.1	3	7.1	9	6.8	67	7.8
	41 - 50	23	6.5	7	5.0	7	5.3	2	6.3	0	0.0	7	5.3	50	5.8
	51 - 60	13	3.7	2	1.4	7	5.3	0	0.0	1	2.4	7	5.3	31	3.6

Item	Survey question	Extended orientation seminar		Academic seminar: uniform content		Academic seminar: various topics		Preprofessional or discipline-linked seminar		Basic study skills seminar		Hybrid		Total	
		n	%	n	%	n	%	n	%	n	%	n	%	n	%
Q16	Approximate number of sections seminar type will be offered in the 2009/2010 academic year:														
	61 - 70	13	3.7	5	3.6	6	4.5	1	3.1	0	0.0	1	0.8	26	3.0
	71 - 80	9	2.5	1	0.7	4	3.0	0	0.0	0	0.0	1	0.8	15	1.7
	81 - 90	6	1.7	2	1.4	1	0.8	0	0.0	0	0.0	2	1.5	11	1.3
	91 - 100	8	2.3	0	0.0	2	1.5	0	0.0	1	2.4	0	0.0	11	1.3
	Over 100	21	5.9	6	4.3	9	6.8	2	6.3	1	2.4	7	5.3	47	5.5
	Total	354	100.0	139	100.0	133	100.0	32	100.0	42	100.0	132	100.0	862	100.0
Q17	Approximate class size for each first-year seminar section?														
	10 students or fewer	6	1.7	0	0.0	1	0.8	0	0.0	2	4.8	1	0.8	13	1.5
	11 - 15	39	11.1	21	15.1	44	33.1	5	16.7	8	19.1	18	13.6	137	16.0
	16 - 19	66	18.9	36	25.9	45	33.8	6	20.0	6	14.3	50	37.9	216	25.3
	20 - 24	134	38.3	47	33.8	33	24.8	7	23.3	15	35.7	35	26.5	282	33.0
	25 - 29	71	20.3	20	14.4	8	6.0	6	20.0	7	16.7	19	14.4	134	15.7
	30 or more	34	9.7	15	10.8	2	1.5	6	20.0	4	9.5	9	6.8	73	8.5
	Total	350	100.0	139	100.0	133	100.0	30	100.0	42	100.0	132	100.0	855	100.0
Q18	Approximate percentage of first-year students required to take the first-year seminar?														
	None	75	21.4	20	14.4	33	24.8	3	10.0	11	26.2	22	16.7	168	19.6
	Less than 10%	27	7.7	7	5.0	4	3.0	1	3.3	9	21.4	7	5.3	57	6.7
	10% - 19%	18	5.1	3	2.2	3	2.3	4	13.3	4	9.5	5	3.8	38	4.4
	20% - 29%	8	2.3	2	1.4	3	2.3	1	3.3	5	11.9	4	3.0	25	2.9
	30% - 39%	10	2.9	1	0.7	0	0.0	2	6.7	1	2.4	3	2.3	18	2.1

Table continues p. 134

Table continued from p. 133

Item	Survey question	Extended orientation seminar		Academic seminar: uniform content		Academic seminar: various topics		Preprofessional or discipline-linked seminar		Basic study skills seminar		Hybrid		Total	
		n	%	n	%	n	%	n	%	n	%	n	%	n	%
Q18	Approximate percentage of first-year students required to take the first-year seminar? *(continued)*														
	40% - 49%	7	2.0	2	1.4	1	0.8	0	0.0	0	0.0	0	0.0	10	1.2
	50% - 59%	4	1.1	2	1.4	0	0.0	2	6.7	0	0.0	1	0.8	10	1.2
	60% - 69%	8	2.3	0	0.0	0	0.0	3	10.0	1	2.4	1	0.8	13	1.5
	70% - 79%	9	2.6	2	1.4	3	2.3	2	6.7	0	0.0	3	2.3	20	2.3
	80% - 89%	15	4.3	5	3.6	1	0.8	1	3.3	0	0.0	4	3.0	27	3.2
	90% - 99%	47	13.4	28	20.1	14	10.5	5	16.7	3	7.1	30	22.7	130	15.2
	100%	122	34.9	67	48.2	71	53.4	6	20.0	8	19.1	52	39.4	339	39.6
	Total	350	100.0	139	100.0	133	100.0	30	100.0	42	100.0	132	100.0	855	100.0
Q19	Which students, by category, are required to take the first-year seminar?														
	None are required to take it	68	19.2	20	14.4	33	24.8	3	9.4	12	28.6	20	15.2	161	18.1
	All first-year students are required to take it	181	51.1	96	69.1	84	63.2	12	37.5	10	23.8	83	62.9	481	54.0
	Academically underprepared students	56	15.8	18	13.0	8	6.0	4	12.5	17	40.5	20	15.2	128	14.4
	First-generation students	20	5.7	9	6.5	4	3.0	1	3.1	0	0.0	9	6.8	45	5.1
	Honors students	25	7.1	11	7.9	8	6.0	3	9.4	1	2.4	7	5.3	56	6.3
	International students	14	4.0	9	6.5	2	1.5	3	9.4	0	0.0	6	4.6	35	3.9
	Learning community participants	30	8.5	10	7.2	9	6.8	4	12.5	2	4.8	6	4.6	64	7.2

Item	Survey question	Extended orientation seminar		Academic seminar: uniform content		Academic seminar: various topics		Preprofessional or discipline-linked seminar		Basic study skills seminar		Hybrid		Total	
		n	%	*n*	%	*n*	%	*n*	%	*n*	%	*n*	%	*n*	%
Q19	Which students, by category, are required to take the first-year seminar? *(continued)*														
	Preprofessional students	9	2.5	7	5.0	4	3.0	2	6.3	0	0.0	4	3.0	27	3.0
	Provisionally admitted students	34	9.6	10	7.2	4	3.0	3	9.4	2	4.8	7	5.3	62	7.0
	Student-athletes	37	10.5	9	6.5	6	4.5	1	3.1	0	0.0	10	7.6	65	7.3
	Students participating in dual-enrollment programs	5	1.4	5	3.6	1	0.8	0	0.0	1	2.4	2	1.5	15	1.7
	Students residing within a particular residence hall	12	3.4	4	2.9	1	0.8	0	0.0	0	0.0	2	1.5	20	2.3
	Students within specific majors	23	6.5	8	5.8	3	2.3	11	34.4	3	7.1	4	3.0	52	5.8
	Transfer students	16	4.5	9	6.5	6	4.5	0	0.0	2	4.8	10	7.6	46	5.2
	TRIO participants	21	5.9	3	2.2	5	3.8	1	3.1	2	4.8	2	1.5	35	3.9
	Undeclared students	18	5.1	9	6.5	6	4.5	0	0.0	0	0.0	7	5.3	41	4.6
	Other (please specify)	51	14.4	10	7.2	9	6.8	2	6.3	7	16.7	15	11.4	99	11.1
Q20	Please identify unique subpopulations of students for which special sections of the first-year seminar are offered:														
	No special sections are offered	142	40.1	69	49.6	67	50.4	8	25.0	17	40.5	60	45.5	381	42.8
	Academically underprepared students	61	17.2	27	19.4	21	15.8	6	18.8	16	38.1	20	15.2	154	17.3

Table continues p. 136

Table continued from p. 135

Item	Survey question	Extended orientation seminar		Academic seminar: uniform content		Academic seminar: various topics		Preprofessional or discipline-linked seminar		Basic study skills seminar		Hybrid		Total	
		n	%	*n*	%	*n*	%	*n*	%	*n*	%	*n*	%	*n*	%
Q20	Please identify unique subpopulations of students for which special sections of the first-year seminar are offered: *(continued)*														
	First-generation students	12	3.4	5	3.6	2	1.5	1	3.1	3	7.1	3	2.3	26	2.9
	Honors students	76	21.5	21	15.1	36	27.1	4	12.5	3	7.1	32	24.2	172	19.3
	International students	13	3.7	4	2.9	4	3.0	5	15.6	2	4.8	5	3.8	35	3.9
	Learning community participants	81	22.9	19	13.7	19	14.3	8	25.0	9	21.4	18	13.6	155	17.4
	Preprofessional students (e.g., prelaw, premed)	23	6.5	5	3.6	6	4.5	5	15.6	0	0.0	6	4.6	45	5.1
	Provisionally admitted students	18	5.1	7	5.0	2	1.5	2	6.3	1	2.4	5	3.8	35	3.9
	Student-athletes	44	12.4	5	3.6	4	3.0	3	9.4	1	2.4	10	7.6	67	7.5
	Students participating in dual-enrollment programs	6	1.7	3	2.2	0	0.0	0	0.0	1	2.4	4	3.0	15	1.7
	Students residing within a particular residence hall	15	4.2	4	2.9	8	6.0	0	0.0	0	0.0	1	0.8	28	3.2
	Students within specific majors	57	16.1	14	10.1	9	6.8	11	34.4	4	9.5	20	15.2	116	13.0
	Transfer students	26	7.3	7	5.0	5	3.8	2	6.3	0	0.0	9	6.8	51	5.7
	TRIO participants	22	6.2	5	3.6	6	4.5	1	3.1	4	9.5	3	2.3	41	4.6
	Undeclared students	28	7.9	7	5.0	3	2.3	8	25.0	1	2.4	9	6.8	56	6.3
	Other (please specify)	39	11.0	12	8.6	8	6.0	0	0.0	4	9.5	14	10.6	81	9.1

Item	Survey question	Extended orientation seminar		Academic seminar: uniform content		Academic seminar: various topics		Preprofessional or discipline-linked seminar		Basic study skills seminar		Hybrid		Total	
		n	%	*n*	%	*n*	%	*n*	%	*n*	%	*n*	%	*n*	%
Q21	Who teaches the first-year seminar?														
	Adjunct faculty	183	51.7	69	49.6	55	41.4	9	28.1	27	64.3	56	42.4	409	46.0
	Full-time non-tenure-track faculty	189	53.4	87	62.6	85	63.9	20	62.5	15	35.7	73	55.3	484	54.4
	Graduate students	28	7.9	4	2.9	4	3.0	3	9.4	2	4.8	9	6.8	50	5.6
	Student affairs professionals	216	61.0	65	46.8	34	25.6	15	46.9	14	33.3	70	53.0	429	48.2
	Tenure-track faculty	193	54.5	95	68.4	120	90.2	22	68.8	15	35.7	89	67.4	546	61.4
	Undergraduate students	23	6.5	3	2.2	2	1.5	4	12.5	1	2.4	10	7.6	45	5.1
	Other campus professionals	127	35.9	37	26.6	27	20.3	11	34.4	8	19.1	44	33.3	266	29.9
Q22	If undergraduate students assist in the first-year seminar, what is their role?														
	They teach independently	5	21.7	0	0.0	1	50.0	2	50.0	0	0.0	4	40.0	13	28.9
	They teach as a part of a team	14	60.9	2	66.7	2	100.0	3	75.0	1	100.0	9	90.0	31	68.9
	They assist the instructor, but do not teach	6	26.1	1	33.3	0	0.0	1	25.0	0	0.0	2	20.0	10	22.2
	Other (please specify)	3	13.0	0	0.0	0	0.0	0	0.0	0	0.0	3	30.0	7	15.6

Table continues p. 138

Table continued from p. 137

Item	Survey question	Extended orientation seminar		Academic seminar: uniform content		Academic seminar: various topics		Preprofessional or discipline-linked seminar		Basic study skills seminar		Hybrid		Total	
		n	%	*n*	%	*n*	%	*n*	%	*n*	%	*n*	%	*n*	%
Q23	Approximate percentage of sections that are team taught														
	No sections	197	56.5	93	66.9	54	40.6	14	46.7	24	58.5	87	65.9	481	56.4
	Less than 10%	70	20.1	21	15.1	55	41.4	8	26.7	8	19.5	17	12.9	187	21.9
	10% - 19%	11	3.2	5	3.6	9	6.8	3	10.0	2	4.9	5	3.8	38	4.5
	20% - 29%	8	2.3	4	2.9	2	1.5	0	0.0	2	4.9	0	0.0	16	1.9
	30% - 39%	5	1.4	2	1.4	4	3.0	0	0.0	0	0.0	3	2.3	14	1.6
	40% - 49%	2	0.6	0	0.0	0	0.0	0	0.0	0	0.0	0	0.0	2	0.2
	50% - 59%	5	1.4	1	0.7	3	2.3	1	3.3	0	0.0	3	2.3	16	1.9
	60% - 69%	2	0.6	0	0.0	0	0.0	0	0.0	0	0.0	0	0.0	2	0.2
	70% - 79%	3	0.9	1	0.7	1	0.8	1	3.3	0	0.0	0	0.0	6	0.7
	80% - 89%	1	0.3	0	0.0	0	0.0	0	0.0	0	0.0	1	0.8	3	0.4
	90% - 99%	8	2.3	1	0.7	1	0.8	1	3.3	0	0.0	4	3.0	15	1.8
	100%	37	10.6	11	7.9	4	3.0	2	6.7	5	12.2	12	9.1	73	8.6
	Total	349	100.0	139	100.0	133	100.0	30	100.0	41	100.0	132	100.0	853	100.0
Q25	Are any first-year students intentionally placed in sections taught by their academic advisors?														
	I don't know	28	8.0	17	12.2	5	3.8	4	13.3	4	9.8	6	4.6	68	8.0
	No	217	62.2	83	59.7	75	56.4	16	53.3	27	65.9	81	61.8	518	60.8
	Yes	104	29.8	39	28.1	53	39.9	10	33.3	10	24.4	44	33.6	266	31.2
	Total	349	100.0	139	100.0	133	100.0	30	100.0	41	100.0	131	100.0	852	100.0

Item	Survey question	Extended orientation seminar		Academic seminar: uniform content		Academic seminar: various topics		Preprofessional or discipline-linked seminar		Basic study skills seminar		Hybrid		Total	
		n	%	*n*	%	*n*	%	*n*	%	*n*	%	*n*	%	*n*	%
Q26	Approximate percentage of students placed in sections with their academic advisors?														
	Less than 10%	17	16.4	7	18.0	6	11.3	1	10.0	4	40.0	10	22.7	47	17.7
	10% - 19%	20	19.2	3	7.7	3	5.7	2	20.0	2	20.0	2	4.6	32	12.0
	20% - 29%	9	8.7	2	5.1	5	9.4	2	20.0	3	30.0	6	13.6	28	10.5
	30% - 39%	6	5.8	2	5.1	3	5.7	2	20.0	0	0.0	3	6.8	16	6.0
	40% - 49%	7	6.7	1	2.6	3	5.7	1	10.0	0	0.0	2	4.6	14	5.3
	50% - 59%	8	7.7	1	2.6	2	3.8	0	0.0	1	10.0	1	2.3	14	5.3
	60% - 69%	3	2.9	1	2.6	3	5.7	0	0.0	0	0.0	1	2.3	8	3.0
	70% - 79%	1	1.0	2	5.1	1	1.9	1	10.0	0	0.0	0	0.0	5	1.9
	80% - 89%	1	1.0	0	0.0	2	3.8	1	10.0	0	0.0	2	4.6	7	2.6
	90% - 99%	9	8.7	3	7.7	2	3.8	0	0.0	0	0.0	4	9.1	18	6.8
	100%	23	22.1	17	43.6	23	43.4	0	0.0	0	0.0	13	29.6	77	28.9
	Total	104	100.0	39	100.0	53	100.0	10	100.0	10	100.0	44	100.0	266	100.0
Q27	Faculty who teach the first-year seminar teach the course as:														
	An overload course	123	63.7	47	49.5	41	34.2	9	40.9	5	33.3	45	50.6	274	50.2
	Part of regular teaching load	92	47.7	75	78.9	106	88.3	19	86.4	12	80.0	54	60.7	368	67.4
	Other (please specify)	34	17.6	5	5.3	8	6.7	1	4.5	2	13.3	11	12.4	61	11.2

Table continues p. 140

Table continued from p. 139

Item	Survey question	Extended orientation seminar		Academic seminar: uniform content		Academic seminar: various topics		Preprofessional or discipline-linked seminar		Basic study skills seminar		Hybrid		Total	
		n	%	n	%	n	%	n	%	n	%	n	%	n	%
Q28	Graduate students who teach the first-year seminar teach the course as:														
	An assigned responsibility	13	46.4	1	25.0	4	100.0	3	100.0	1	50.0	4	44.4	26	52.0
	An extra responsibility	12	42.9	3	75.0	0	0.0	1	33.3	1	50.0	5	55.6	22	44.0
	Other (please specify)	6	21.4	0	0.0	1	25.0	0	0.0	0	0.0	3	33.3	10	20.0
Q29	Student affairs professionals who teach the first-year seminar teach the course as:														
	An assigned responsibility	71	32.9	14	21.5	5	14.7	7	46.7	9	64.3	19	27.1	127	29.6
	An extra responsibility	156	72.2	50	76.9	29	85.3	8	53.3	8	57.1	50	71.4	315	73.4
	Other (please specify)	27	12.5	12	18.5	3	8.8	3	20.0	0	0.0	10	14.3	56	13.1
Q30	Type of compensation is offered to adjunct faculty for teaching the first-year seminar?														
	No compensation is offered	22	12.0	11	15.9	12	21.8	4	44.4	3	11.1	4	7.1	56	13.7
	Graduate student support	1	0.6	0	0.0	0	0.0	1	11.1	0	0.0	0	0.0	2	0.5
	Release time	3	1.6	1	1.5	2	3.6	0	0.0	1	3.7	0	0.0	8	2.0
	Stipend	100	54.6	37	53.6	28	50.9	4	44.4	11	40.7	30	53.6	215	52.6
	Unrestricted professional development funds	3	1.6	0	0.0	1	1.8	0	0.0	1	3.7	0	0.0	6	1.5
	Other (please specify)	62	33.9	22	31.9	18	32.7	2	22.2	13	48.2	23	41.1	144	35.2

Item	Survey question	Extended orientation seminar		Academic seminar: uniform content		Academic seminar: various topics		Preprofessional or discipline-linked seminar		Basic study skills seminar		Hybrid		Total	
		n	%	n	%	n	%	n	%	n	%	n	%	n	%
Q31	Type of compensation is offered to tenure faculty for teaching the first-year seminar?														
	No compensation is offered	52	26.9	35	36.8	62	51.7	14	63.6	4	26.7	26	29.2	195	35.7
	Graduate student support	1	0.5	0	0.0	0	0.0	1	4.6	0	0.0	0	0.0	2	0.4
	Release time	9	4.7	5	5.3	8	6.7	0	0.0	0	0.0	5	5.6	28	5.1
	Stipend	88	45.6	32	33.7	30	25.0	5	22.7	4	26.7	42	47.2	203	37.2
	Unrestricted professional development funds	7	3.6	0	0.0	7	5.8	0	0.0	0	0.0	0	0.0	14	2.6
	Other (please specify)	53	27.5	33	34.7	33	27.5	4	18.2	7	46.7	22	24.7	159	29.1
Q32	Type of compensation is offered to student affairs professionals for teaching the first-year seminar?														
	No compensation is offered	79	36.6	16	24.6	11	32.4	6	40.0	4	28.6	27	38.6	148	34.5
	Graduate student support	1	0.5	0	0.0	0	0.0	0	0.0	1	7.1	0	0.0	2	0.5
	Release time	13	6.0	2	3.1	3	8.8	1	6.7	0	0.0	2	2.9	23	5.4
	Stipend	98	45.4	36	55.4	16	47.1	5	33.3	5	35.7	34	48.6	201	46.9
	Unrestricted professional development funds	5	2.3	0	0.0	2	5.9	0	0.0	0	0.0	0	0.0	8	1.9
	Other (please specify)	47	21.8	15	23.1	7	20.6	4	26.7	7	50.0	13	18.6	95	22.1

Table continues p. 142

Table continued from p. 141

Item	Survey question	Extended orientation seminar		Academic seminar: uniform content		Academic seminar: various topics		Preprofessional or discipline-linked seminar		Basic study skills seminar		Hybrid		Total	
		n	%	*n*	%	*n*	%	*n*	%	*n*	%	*n*	%	*n*	%
Q33	Type of compensation is offered to other campus professionals for teaching the first-year seminar?														
	No compensation is offered	44	34.7	11	29.7	8	29.6	6	54.6	1	12.5	15	34.1	89	33.5
	Graduate student support	1	0.8	0	0.0	0	0.0	0	0.0	0	0.0	0	0.0	1	0.4
	Release time	4	3.2	3	8.1	3	11.1	0	0.0	0	0.0	0	0.0	11	4.1
	Stipend	54	42.5	19	51.4	11	40.7	3	27.3	4	50.0	21	47.7	118	44.4
	Unrestricted professional development funds	4	3.2	0	0.0	0	0.0	0	0.0	0	0.0	0	0.0	4	1.5
	Other (please specify)	36	28.4	11	29.7	8	29.6	4	36.4	4	50.0	11	25.0	76	28.6
Q34	Type of compensation is offered to graduate students for teaching the first-year seminar?														
	No compensation is offered	10	35.7	1	25.0	2	50.0	3	100.0	1	50.0	1	11.1	18	36.0
	Stipend	14	50.0	3	75.0	3	75.0	2	66.7	0	0.0	5	55.6	27	54.0
	Other(please specify)	8	28.6	0	0.0	1	25.0	0	0.0	1	50.0	3	3.3	13	26.0
Q35	Amount of stipend per class for adjunct faculty:														
	$500 or less	11	11.0	2	5.4	0	0.0	1	25.0	2	18.2	5	16.1	22	10.2
	$501 - $1,000	33	33.0	6	16.2	3	10.7	1	25.0	0	0.0	8	25.8	52	24.1
	$1,001 - $1,500	16	16.0	6	16.2	1	3.6	0	0.0	1	9.1	7	22.6	32	14.8
	$1,501 - $2,000	18	18.0	6	16.2	3	10.7	0	0.0	5	45.5	5	16.1	38	17.6

Item	Survey question	Extended orientation seminar		Academic seminar: uniform content		Academic seminar: various topics		Preprofessional or discipline-linked seminar		Basic study skills seminar		Hybrid		Total	
		n	%	n	%	n	%	n	%	n	%	n	%	n	%
Q35	Amount of stipend per class for adjunct faculty: (continued)														
	$2,001 - $2,500	13	13.0	6	16.2	5	17.9	0	0.0	3	27.3	1	3.2	29	13.4
	$2,501 - $3,000	6	6.0	6	16.2	6	21.4	2	50.0	0	0.0	3	9.7	23	10.6
	$3,001 - $3,500	2	2.0	2	5.4	1	3.6	0	0.0	0	0.0	1	3.2	6	2.8
	$3,501 - $4,000	0	0.0	0	0.0	3	10.7	0	0.0	0	0.0	0	0.0	3	1.4
	$4,001 - $4,500	1	1.0	1	2.7	6	21.4	0	0.0	0	0.0	1	3.2	9	4.2
	$4,501 - $5,000	0	0.0	1	2.7	0	0.0	0	0.0	0	0.0	0	0.0	1	0.5
	More than $5,000	0	0.0	1	2.7	0	0.0	0	0.0	0	0.0	0	0.0	1	0.5
	Total	100	100.0	37	100.0	28	100.0	4	100.0	11	100.0	31	100.0	216	100.0
Q36	Amount of stipend per class for tenure-track faculty:														
	$500 or less	14	15.9	4	12.5	1	3.3	2	40.0	0	0.0	5	11.6	26	12.7
	$501 - $1,000	32	36.4	11	34.4	7	23.3	0	0.0	1	25.0	13	30.2	66	32.4
	$1,001 - $1,500	14	15.9	5	15.6	7	23.3	0	0.0	1	25.0	8	18.6	35	17.2
	$1,501 - $2,000	10	11.4	7	21.9	0	0.0	2	40.0	0	0.0	8	18.6	27	13.2
	$2,001 - $2,500	6	6.8	3	9.4	3	10.0	0	0.0	1	25.0	5	11.6	18	8.8
	$2,501 - $3,000	8	9.1	1	3.1	3	10.0	1	20.0	0	0.0	2	4.7	15	7.4
	$3,001 - $3,500	4	4.6	0	0.0	0	0.0	0	0.0	0	0.0	1	2.3	5	2.5
	$3,501 - $4,000	0	0.0	0	0.0	5	16.7	0	0.0	1	25.0	0	0.0	6	2.9
	$4,001 - $4,500	0	0.0	0	0.0	2	6.7	0	0.0	0	0.0	0	0.0	2	1.0
	$4,501 - $5,000	0	0.0	0	0.0	0	0.0	0	0.0	0	0.0	1	2.3	1	0.5
	More than $5,000	0	0.0	1	3.1	2	6.7	0	0.0	0	0.0	0	0.0	3	1.5
	Total	88	100.0	32	100.0	30	100.0	5	100.0	4	100.0	43	100.0	204	100.0

Table continues p. 144

Table continued from p. 143

Item	Survey question	Extended orientation seminar		Academic seminar: uniform content		Academic seminar: various topics		Preprofessional or discipline-linked seminar		Basic study skills seminar		Hybrid		Total	
		n	%	n	%	n	%	n	%	n	%	n	%	n	%
Q37	Amount of stipend per class for student affairs professionals:														
	$500 or less	14	14.3	5	13.9	0	0.0	2	40.0	1	20.0	6	17.1	29	14.4
	$501 - $1,000	39	39.8	11	30.6	4	25.0	1	20.0	3	60.0	9	25.7	69	34.2
	$1,001 - $1,500	18	18.4	5	13.9	4	25.0	1	20.0	1	20.0	4	11.4	34	16.8
	$1,501 - $2,000	13	13.3	4	11.1	1	6.3	1	20.0	0	0.0	9	25.7	30	14.9
	$2,001 - $2,500	6	6.1	7	19.4	2	12.5	0	0.0	0	0.0	2	5.7	18	8.9
	$2,501 - $3,000	6	6.1	4	11.1	4	25.0	0	0.0	0	0.0	3	8.6	17	8.4
	$3,001 - $3,500	2	2.0	0	0.0	0	0.0	0	0.0	0	0.0	1	2.9	3	1.5
	$3,501 - $4,000	0	0.0	0	0.0	1	6.3	0	0.0	0	0.0	0	0.0	1	0.5
	$4,001 - $4,500	0	0.0	0	0.0	0	0.0	0	0.0	0	0.0	1	2.9	1	0.5
	$4,501 - $5,000	0	0.0	0	0.0	0	0.0	0	0.0	0	0.0	0	0.0	0	0.0
	More than $5,000	0	0.0	0	0.0	0	0.0	0	0.0	0	0.0	0	0.0	0	0.0
	Total	98	100.0	36	100.0	16	100.0	5	100.0	5	100.0	35	100.0	202	100.0
Q38	Amount of stipend per class for other campus professionals:														
	$500 or less	12	22.2	1	5.3	0	0.0	1	33.3	0	0.0	2	9.1	16	13.4
	$501 - $1,000	16	29.6	7	36.8	2	18.2	1	33.3	1	25.0	4	18.2	33	27.7
	$1,001 - $1,500	10	18.5	1	5.3	1	9.1	0	0.0	2	50.0	3	13.6	17	14.3
	$1,501 - $2,000	6	11.1	3	15.8	2	18.2	1	33.3	0	0.0	9	40.9	24	20.2
	$2,001 - $2,500	5	9.3	5	26.3	2	18.2	0	0.0	1	25.0	1	4.6	15	12.6
	$2,501 - $3,000	4	7.4	1	5.3	1	9.1	0	0.0	0	0.0	2	9.1	8	6.7

Item	Survey question	Extended orientation seminar		Academic seminar: uniform content		Academic seminar: various topics		Preprofessional or discipline-linked seminar		Basic study skills seminar		Hybrid		Total	
		n	%	n	%	n	%	n	%	n	%	n	%	n	%
Q38	Amount of stipend per class for other campus professionals: *(continued)*														
	$3,001 - $3,500	1	1.9	0	0.0	0	0.0	0	0.0	0	0.0	0	0.0	1	0.8
	$3,501 - $4,000	0	0.0	0	0.0	1	9.1	0	0.0	0	0.0	0	0.0	1	0.8
	$4,001 - $4,500	0	0.0	0	0.0	2	18.2	0	0.0	0	0.0	1	4.6	3	2.5
	$4,501 - $5,000	0	0.0	0	0.0	0	0.0	0	0.0	0	0.0	0	0.0	0	0.0
	More than $5,000	0	0.0	1	5.3	0	0.0	0	0.0	0	0.0	0	0.0	1	0.8
	Total	54	100.0	19	100.0	11	100.0	3	100.0	4	100.0	22	100.0	119	100.0
Q39	Amount of stipend per class for graduate students:														
	$500 or less	8	57.1	1	33.3	0	0.0	0	0.0	0	0.0	1	20.0	10	37.0
	$501 - $1,000	4	28.6	1	33.3	0	0.0	1	50.0	0	0.0	1	20.0	6	22.2
	$1,001 - $1,500	2	14.3	0	0.0	1	33.3	0	0.0	0	0.0	2	40.0	6	22.2
	$1,501 - $2,000	0	0.0	0	0.0	1	33.3	0	0.0	0	0.0	1	20.0	2	7.4
	$2,001 - $2,500	0	0.0	0	0.0	1	33.3	0	0.0	0	0.0	0	0.0	1	3.7
	$2,501 - $3,000	0	0.0	0	0.0	0	0.0	0	0.0	0	0.0	0	0.0	0	0.0
	$3,001 - $3,500	0	0.0	0	0.0	0	0.0	0	0.0	0	0.0	0	0.0	0	0.0
	$3,501 - $4,000	0	0.0	0	0.0	0	0.0	0	0.0	0	0.0	0	0.0	0	0.0
	$4,001 - $4,500	0	0.0	1	33.3	0	0.0	0	0.0	0	0.0	0	0.0	1	3.7
	$4,501 - $5,000	0	0.0	0	0.0	0	0.0	0	0.0	0	0.0	0	0.0	0	0.0
	More than $5,000	0	0.0	0	0.0	0	0.0	1	50.0	0	0.0	0	0.0	1	3.7
	Total	14	100.0	3	100.0	3	100.0	2	100.0	0	100.0	5	100.0	27	100.0

Table continues p. 146

Table continued from p. 145

Item	Survey question	Extended orientation seminar		Academic seminar: uniform content		Academic seminar: various topics		Preprofessional or discipline-linked seminar		Basic study skills seminar		Hybrid		Total	
		n	%	n	%	n	%	n	%	n	%	n	%	n	%
Q43	Is instructor training offered for first-year seminar instructors?														
	I don't know	9	2.6	9	6.5	2	1.5	2	6.7	2	4.9	2	1.5	26	3.1
	No	62	17.9	23	16.6	30	22.7	10	33.3	16	39.0	26	19.9	177	20.8
	Yes	276	79.5	107	77.0	100	75.8	18	60.0	23	56.1	103	78.6	646	76.1
	Total	347	100.0	139	100.0	132	100.0	30	100.0	41	100.0	131	100.0	849	100.0
Q44	Is instructor training required for first-year seminar instructors?														
	I don't know	13	3.8	11	7.9	1	0.8	2	6.7	4	9.8	1	0.8	33	3.9
	No	135	38.9	53	38.1	85	64.4	23	76.7	24	58.5	55	42.0	391	46.1
	Yes	199	57.4	75	54.0	46	34.9	5	16.7	13	31.7	75	57.3	425	50.1
	Total	347	100.0	139	100.0	132	100.0	30	100.0	41	100.0	131	100.0	849	100.0
Q45	How long is new instructor training?														
	Half a day or less	113	40.9	36	33.6	26	26.0	7	38.9	11	47.8	36	35.0	237	36.7
	1 day	64	23.2	21	19.6	23	23.0	2	11.1	4	17.4	24	23.3	140	21.7
	2 days	32	11.6	11	10.3	13	13.0	1	5.6	3	13.0	11	10.7	74	11.5
	3 days	13	4.7	7	6.5	1	1.0	2	11.1	0	0.0	8	7.8	33	5.1
	4 days	2	0.7	1	0.9	4	4.0	0	0.0	1	4.4	0	0.0	8	1.2
	1 week	5	1.8	4	3.7	4	4.0	0	0.0	1	4.4	6	5.8	20	3.1
	Other	47	17.0	27	25.2	29	29.0	6	33.3	3	13.0	18	17.5	134	20.7
	Total	276	100.0	107	100.0	100	100.0	18	100.0	23	100.0	103	100.0	646	100.0

Item	Survey question	Extended orientation seminar		Academic seminar: uniform content		Academic seminar: various topics		Preprofessional or discipline-linked seminar		Basic study skills seminar		Hybrid		Total	
		n	%	n	%	n	%	n	%	n	%	n	%	n	%
Q46	Typical length of a section of the first-year seminar:														
	Half a semester	63	18.2	12	8.6	4	3.1	4	13.3	4	9.8	13	9.9	107	12.6
	One quarter	24	6.9	8	5.8	4	3.1	4	13.3	5	12.2	4	3.1	50	5.9
	One semester	201	57.9	96	69.1	113	86.3	18	60.0	31	75.6	98	74.8	575	67.8
	One year	8	2.3	12	8.6	3	2.3	1	3.3	0	0.0	6	4.6	32	3.8
	Other	51	14.7	11	7.9	7	5.3	3	10.0	1	2.4	10	7.6	84	9.9
	Total	347	100.0	139	100.0	131	100.0	30	100.0	41	100.0	131	100.0	848	100.0
Q47	How is the first-year seminar graded?														
	Pass/fail	59	17.0	8	5.8	4	3.1	8	26.7	7	17.1	20	15.3	110	13.0
	Letter grade	261	75.2	125	89.9	117	89.3	18	60.0	31	75.6	108	82.4	683	80.5
	No grade	15	4.3	2	1.4	1	0.8	0	0.0	1	2.4	0	0.0	21	2.5
	Other	12	3.5	4	2.9	9	6.9	4	13.3	2	4.9	3	2.3	34	4.0
	Total	347	100.0	139	100.0	131	100.0	30	100.0	41	100.0	131	100.0	848	100.0
Q48	Does the first-year seminar carry academic credit?														
	I dont know	1	0.3	0	0.0	0	0.0	0	0.0	0	0.0	0	0.0	2	0.2
	No	44	12.7	6	4.3	2	1.5	0	0.0	8	19.5	7	5.3	72	8.5
	Yes	302	87.0	133	95.7	129	98.5	30	100.0	33	80.5	124	94.7	774	91.3
	Total	347	100.0	139	100.0	131	100.0	30	100.0	41	100.0	131	100.0	848	100.0
Q49	How many credits does the first-year seminar carry?														
	1	179	59.3	41	30.8	20	15.5	17	56.7	6	18.2	59	47.6	335	43.3
	2	54	17.9	17	12.8	7	5.4	4	13.3	6	18.2	19	15.3	109	14.1

Table continues p. 148

Table continued from p. 147

Item	Survey question	Extended orientation seminar		Academic seminar: uniform content		Academic seminar: various topics		Preprofessional or discipline-linked seminar		Basic study skills seminar		Hybrid		Total	
		n	%	n	%	n	%	n	%	n	%	n	%	n	%
Q49	How many credits does the first-year seminar carry? *(continued)*														
	3	65	21.5	57	42.9	57	44.2	7	23.3	19	57.6	36	29.0	247	31.9
	4	3	1.0	11	8.3	38	29.5	1	3.3	0	0.0	10	8.1	65	8.4
	5	1	0.3	0	0.0	1	0.8	0	0.0	1	3.0	0	0.0	3	0.4
	More than 5	0	0.0	7	5.3	6	4.7	1	3.3	1	3.0	0	0.0	15	1.9
	Total	302	100.0	133	100.0	129	100.0	30	100.0	33	100.0	124	100.0	774	100.0
Q50	How is the first-year seminar credit applied? (Check all that apply)														
	As an elective	153	50.7	34	25.6	34	26.4	9	30.0	22	66.7	44	35.5	308	39.8
	Toward general education requirements	124	41.1	86	64.7	97	75.2	14	46.7	9	27.3	70	56.5	411	53.1
	Toward major requirements	25	8.3	9	6.8	16	12.4	15	50.0	0	0.0	9	7.3	75	9.7
	Other (please specify)	28	9.3	12	9.0	12	9.3	4	13.3	3	9.1	12	9.7	73	9.4
Q51	Total classroom contact hours per week:														
	1	125	36.0	26	18.7	10	7.6	11	36.7	6	14.6	41	31.3	226	26.7
	2	111	32.0	33	23.7	14	10.7	8	26.7	5	12.2	34	26.0	215	25.4
	3	90	25.9	65	46.8	89	67.9	6	20.0	25	61.0	45	34.4	329	38.8
	4	9	2.6	8	5.8	17	13.0	3	10.0	2	4.9	9	6.9	51	6.0
	More than 5	12	3.5	7	5.0	1	0.8	2	6.7	3	7.3	2	1.5	27	3.2
	Total	347	100.0	139	100.0	131	100.0	30	100.0	41	100.0	131	100.0	848	100.0

Item	Survey question	Extended orientation seminar		Academic seminar: uniform content		Academic seminar: various topics		Preprofessional or discipline-linked seminar		Basic study skills seminar		Hybrid		Total	
		n	%	n	%	n	%	n	%	n	%	n	%	n	%
Q52	Do any sections include a service-learning component?														
	I don't know	24	6.9	10	7.2	7	5.3	5	16.7	3	7.3	6	4.6	57	6.7
	No	207	59.7	72	51.8	51	38.9	12	40.0	30	73.2	64	48.9	449	52.9
	Yes	116	33.4	57	41.0	73	55.7	13	43.3	8	19.5	61	46.6	342	40.3
	Total	347	100.0	139	100.0	131	100.0	30	100.0	41	100.0	131	100.0	848	100.0
Q54	Are any sections linked to one or more other courses?														
	I don't know	6	1.7	3	2.2	2	1.5	2	6.7	0	0.0	0	0.0	13	1.5
	No	204	58.8	89	64.0	87	66.4	17	56.7	24	58.5	91	69.5	532	62.7
	Yes	137	39.5	47	33.8	42	32.1	11	36.7	17	41.5	40	30.5	303	35.7
	Total	347	100.0	139	100.0	131	100.0	30	100.0	41	100.0	131	100.0	848	100.0
Q55	Do any sections incorporate a first-year/summer reading program component?														
	I don't know	4	1.2	2	1.4	1	0.8	0	0.0	2	4.9	3	2.3	12	1.4
	No	248	71.5	86	61.9	80	61.1	18	60.0	31	75.6	87	66.4	573	67.6
	Yes	95	27.4	51	36.7	50	38.2	12	40.0	8	19.5	41	31.3	263	31.0
	Total	347	100.0	139	100.0	131	100.0	30	100.0	41	100.0	131	100.0	848	100.0
Q57	Do any sections incorporate online components?														
	I don't know	22	6.4	14	10.1	13	9.9	6	20.0	6	14.6	9	6.9	71	8.4
	No	131	37.9	54	38.9	59	45.0	8	26.7	16	39.0	47	35.9	328	38.7
	Yes	193	55.8	71	51.1	59	45.0	16	53.3	19	46.3	75	57.3	448	52.9
	Total	346	100.0	139	100.0	131	100.0	30	100.0	41	100.0	131	100.0	847	100.0

Table continues p. 150

Table continued from p. 149

Item	Survey question	Extended orientation seminar		Academic seminar: uniform content		Academic seminar: various topics		Preprofessional or discipline-linked seminar		Basic study skills seminar		Hybrid		Total	
		n	%	n	%	n	%	n	%	n	%	n	%	n	%
Q59	Are there any online-only sections?														
	I don't know	4	1.2	2	1.4	1	0.8	2	6.7	0	0.0	0	0.0	9	1.1
	No	271	78.3	115	82.7	128	97.7	24	80.0	35	85.4	118	90.1	715	84.4
	Yes	71	20.5	22	15.8	2	1.5	4	13.3	6	14.6	13	9.9	123	14.5
	Total	346	100.0	139	100.0	131	100.0	30	100.0	41	100.0	131	100.0	847	100.0
Q60	Approximate percentage of online-only sections:														
	Less than 10%	36	50.7	13	59.1	2	100.0	4	100.0	3	50.0	7	53.9	69	56.1
	10% - 19%	8	11.3	3	13.6	0	0.0	0	0.0	1	16.7	4	30.8	16	13.0
	20% - 29%	8	11.3	3	13.6	0	0.0	0	0.0	2	33.3	1	7.7	15	12.2
	30% - 39%	5	7.0	0	0.0	0	0.0	0	0.0	0	0.0	1	7.7	6	4.9
	40% - 49%	1	1.4	2	9.1	0	0.0	0	0.0	0	0.0	0	0.0	3	2.4
	50% - 59%	4	5.6	0	0.0	0	0.0	0	0.0	0	0.0	0	0.0	4	3.3
	60% - 69%	1	1.4	0	0.0	0	0.0	0	0.0	0	0.0	0	0.0	1	0.8
	70% - 79%	0	0.0	0	0.0	0	0.0	0	0.0	0	0.0	0	0.0	0	0.0
	80% - 89%	1	1.4	0	0.0	0	0.0	0	0.0	0	0.0	0	0.0	1	0.8
	90% - 99%	0	0.0	0	0.0	0	0.0	0	0.0	0	0.0	0	0.0	0	0.0
	100%	7	9.9	1	4.6	0	0.0	0	0.0	0	0.0	0	0.0	8	6.5
	Total	71	100.0	22	100.0	2	100.0	4	100.0	6	100.0	13	100.0	123	100.0
Q61	Campus unit directly administers the first-year seminar?														
	Academic affairs	108	31.2	56	40.3	62	47.3	7	23.3	12	29.3	56	42.8	313	37.0
	Academic department(s)	55	15.9	22	15.8	14	10.7	7	23.3	14	34.2	22	16.8	138	16.3

Item	Survey question	Extended orientation seminar n	%	Academic seminar: uniform content n	%	Academic seminar: various topics n	%	Preprofessional or discipline-linked seminar n	%	Basic study skills seminar n	%	Hybrid n	%	Total n	%
Q61	Campus unit directly administers the first-year seminar? (continued)														
	College or school	18	5.2	9	6.5	19	14.5	11	36.7	1	2.4	8	6.1	67	7.9
	First-year program office	45	13.0	24	17.3	15	11.5	1	3.3	0	0.0	14	10.7	101	11.9
	Student affairs	68	19.7	15	10.8	4	3.1	1	3.3	6	14.6	17	13.0	118	13.9
	Other	52	15.0	13	9.4	17	13.0	3	10.0	8	19.5	14	10.7	110	13.0
	Total	346	100.0	139	100.0	131	100.0	30	100.0	41	100.0	131	100.0	847	100.0
Q62	Is there a dean/director/coordinator of the first-year seminar?														
	I don't know	4	1.2	0	0.0	0	0.0	0	0.0	0	0.0	0	0.0	4	0.5
	No	75	21.7	25	18.0	32	24.4	21	70.0	22	53.7	23	17.6	207	24.4
	Yes	267	77.2	114	82.0	99	75.6	9	30.0	19	46.3	108	82.4	636	75.1
	Total	346	100.0	139	100.0	131	100.0	30	100.0	41	100.0	131	100.0	847	100.0
Q63	Does the dean/director/coordinator of the first-year seminar work full time or less than full time in this position?														
	Less than full time	147	55.1	70	61.4	71	71.7	7	77.8	14	73.7	75	69.4	396	62.3
	Full time (approximately 40 hr/wk)	120	44.9	44	38.6	28	28.3	2	22.2	5	26.3	33	30.6	240	37.8
	Total	267	100.0	114	100.0	99	100.0	9	100.0	19	100.0	108	100.0	636	100.0
Q64	Does the dean/director/coordinator have another position on campus?														
	I don't know	0	0.0	0	0.0	0	0.0	0	0.0	0	0.0	0	0.0	0	0.0
	No	3	2.1	2	2.9	0	0.0	0	0.0	1	7.1	2	2.7	9	2.3
	Yes	143	98.0	67	97.1	71	100.0	7	100.0	13	92.9	73	97.3	385	97.7
	Total	146	100.0	69	100.0	71	100.0	7	100.0	14	100.0	75	100.0	394	100.0

Table continues p. 152

Table continued from p. 151

Item	Survey question	Extended orientation seminar		Academic seminar: uniform content		Academic seminar: various topics		Preprofessional or discipline-linked seminar		Basic study skills seminar		Hybrid		Total	
		n	%	n	%	n	%	n	%	n	%	n	%	n	%
Q65	The dean/director/coordinator's other campus role is as a/an:														
	Academic affairs administrator	48	33.6	11	16.4	24	33.8	4	57.1	2	15.4	19	26.0	110	28.6
	Faculty member	47	32.9	14	20.9	27	38.0	4	57.1	2	15.4	20	27.4	116	30.1
	Student affairs administrator	47	32.9	10	14.9	23	32.4	4	57.1	3	23.1	19	26.0	108	28.1
	Other (please specify)	46	32.2	11	16.4	23	32.4	4	57.1	2	15.4	18	24.7	106	27.5
Q66	Select the three most important course objectives for the first-year seminar:														
	Create common first-year experience	81	22.9	43	30.9	33	24.8	5	15.6	7	16.7	29	22.0	207	23.3
	Develop a connection with the institution	212	59.9	63	45.3	53	39.9	12	37.5	20	47.6	68	51.5	447	50.2
	Develop academic skills	161	45.5	94	67.6	88	66.2	13	40.6	37	88.1	77	58.3	486	54.6
	Develop financial literacy	3	0.9	2	1.4	0	0.0	0	0.0	2	4.8	1	0.8	10	1.1
	Develop support network/friendships	80	22.6	14	10.1	15	11.3	4	12.5	7	16.7	33	25.0	155	17.4
	Develop writing skills	11	3.1	27	19.4	50	37.6	1	3.1	6	14.3	9	6.8	106	11.9
	Improve sophomore return rates	65	18.4	23	16.6	17	12.8	4	12.5	2	4.8	24	18.2	138	15.5
	Increase student/faculty interaction	46	13.0	19	13.7	53	39.9	7	21.9	2	4.8	20	15.2	150	16.9

Item	Survey question	Extended orientation seminar		Academic seminar: uniform content		Academic seminar: various topics		Preprofessional or discipline-linked seminar		Basic study skills seminar		Hybrid		Total	
		n	%	n	%	n	%	n	%	n	%	n	%	n	%
Q66	Select the three most important course objectives for the first-year seminar: (continued)														
	Introduce a discipline	8	2.3	7	5.0	21	15.8	16	50.0	1	2.4	9	6.8	62	7.0
	Provide orientation to campus resources and services	231	65.3	53	38.1	18	13.5	16	50.0	23	54.8	68	51.5	424	47.6
	Self-exploration/ personal development	110	31.1	53	38.1	17	12.8	9	28.1	13	31.0	42	31.8	254	28.5
	Encourage arts participation	0	0.0	2	1.4	2	1.5	0	0.0	0	0.0	1	0.8	5	0.6
	Other (please specify)	22	6.2	14	10.1	19	14.3	2	6.3	2	4.8	10	7.6	72	8.1
Q67	The three most important topics that compose the content of this first-year seminar:														
	Academic planning/ advising	163	46.0	41	29.5	23	17.3	16	50.0	20	47.6	46	34.9	318	35.7
	Career exploration/ preparation	70	19.8	15	10.8	6	4.5	16	50.0	4	9.5	22	16.7	138	15.5
	Campus resources	217	61.3	44	31.7	18	13.5	13	40.6	17	40.5	58	43.9	377	42.4
	College policies and procedures	85	24.0	16	11.5	3	2.3	5	15.6	1	2.4	22	16.7	134	15.1
	Critical thinking	58	16.4	72	51.8	103	77.4	4	12.5	11	26.2	49	37.1	310	34.8
	Diversity issues	20	5.6	19	13.7	10	7.5	1	3.1	1	2.4	9	6.8	61	6.9
	Financial literacy	5	1.4	0	0.0	0	0.0	1	3.1	2	4.8	0	0.0	9	1.0
	Health and wellness	18	5.1	3	2.2	1	0.8	0	0.0	0	0.0	9	6.8	33	3.7
	Relationship issues	35	9.9	17	12.2	4	3.0	1	3.1	0	0.0	18	13.6	82	9.2

Table continues p. 154

Table continued from p. 153

Item	Survey question	Extended orientation seminar		Academic seminar: uniform content		Academic seminar: various topics		Preprofessional or discipline-linked seminar		Basic study skills seminar		Hybrid		Total	
		n	%	n	%	n	%	n	%	n	%	n	%	n	%
	Specific disciplinary topic	5	1.4	13	9.4	70	52.6	15	46.9	1	2.4	19	14.4	125	14.0
	Study skills	164	46.3	56	40.3	20	15.0	5	15.6	35	83.3	60	45.5	354	39.8
	Time management	132	37.3	30	21.6	9	6.8	7	21.9	20	47.6	37	28.0	246	27.6
	Writing skills	18	5.1	40	28.8	70	52.6	1	3.1	4	9.5	17	12.9	154	17.3
	Other (please specify)	36	10.2	31	22.3	31	23.3	2	6.3	5	11.9	22	16.7	132	14.8
Q70	Has your first-year seminar been formally assessed or evaluated since Fall 2006?														
	I don't know	35	10.1	18	13.0	8	6.3	5	16.7	5	12.5	9	6.9	82	9.8
	No	111	32.2	46	33.3	42	32.8	14	46.7	19	47.5	40	30.5	284	33.8
	Yes	199	57.7	74	53.6	78	60.9	11	36.7	16	40.0	82	62.6	475	56.5
	Total	345	100.0	138	100.0	128	100.0	30	100.0	40	100.0	131	100.0	841	100.0
Q71	Analysis of institutional data (e.g., GPA, retention rates, graduation)														
	I don't know	10	5.0	3	4.1	3	3.9	1	9.1	0	0.0	3	3.7	20	4.2
	No	30	15.1	17	23.3	18	23.1	1	9.1	4	25.0	20	24.4	97	20.5
	Yes	159	79.9	53	72.6	57	73.1	9	81.8	12	75.0	59	72.0	357	75.3
	Total	199	100.0	73	100.0	78	100.0	11	100.0	16	100.0	82	100.0	474	100.0
Q72	Focus groups with instructors														
	I don't know	11	5.5	3	4.1	1	1.3	1	9.1	4	25.0	4	4.9	24	5.1
	No	89	44.7	26	35.6	35	44.9	5	45.5	8	50.0	35	42.7	207	43.7
	Yes	99	49.8	44	60.3	42	53.9	5	45.5	4	25.0	43	52.4	243	51.3
	Total	199	100.0	73	100.0	78	100.0	11	100.0	16	100.0	82	100.0	474	100.0

Item	Survey question	Extended orientation seminar		Academic seminar: uniform content		Academic seminar: various topics		Preprofessional or discipline-linked seminar		Basic study skills seminar		Hybrid		Total	
		n	%	n	%	n	%	n	%	n	%	n	%	n	%
Q73	Focus groups with students														
	I don't know	10	5.0	1	1.4	4	5.1	1	9.1	0	0.0	9	11.0	26	5.5
	No	110	55.3	31	42.5	34	43.6	6	54.6	12	75.0	42	51.2	246	51.9
	Yes	79	39.7	41	56.2	40	51.3	4	36.4	4	25.0	31	37.8	202	42.6
	Total	199	100.0	73	100.0	78	100.0	11	100.0	16	100.0	82	100.0	474	100.0
Q74	Individual interviews with instructors														
	I don't know	15	7.5	6	8.2	4	5.1	2	18.2	2	12.5	4	4.9	33	7.0
	No	87	43.7	32	43.8	42	53.9	4	36.4	7	43.8	42	51.2	225	47.5
	Yes	97	48.7	35	48.0	32	41.0	5	45.5	7	43.8	36	43.9	216	45.6
	Total	199	100.0	73	100.0	78	100.0	11	100.0	16	100.0	82	100.0	474	100.0
Q75	Individual interviews with students														
	I don't know	13	6.5	8	11.0	7	9.0	1	9.1	3	18.8	4	4.9	36	7.6
	No	127	63.8	40	54.8	50	64.1	7	63.6	11	68.8	47	57.3	295	62.2
	Yes	59	29.7	25	34.3	21	26.9	3	27.3	2	12.5	31	37.8	143	30.2
	Total	199	100.0	73	100.0	78	100.0	11	100.0	16	100.0	82	100.0	474	100.0
Q76	Student course evaluation														
	I don't know	3	1.5	0	0.0	1	1.3	0	0.0	1	6.3	0	0.0	5	1.1
	No	8	4.0	1	1.4	6	7.7	0	0.0	0	0.0	4	4.9	19	4.0
	Yes	188	94.5	72	98.6	71	91.0	11	100.0	15	93.8	78	95.1	450	94.9
	Total	199	100.0	73	100.0	78	100.0	11	100.0	16	100.0	82	100.0	474	100.0

Table continues p. 156

Table continued from p. 155

Item	Survey question	Extended orientation seminar		Academic seminar: uniform content		Academic seminar: various topics		Preprofessional or discipline-linked seminar		Basic study skills seminar		Hybrid		Total	
		n	%	n	%	n	%	n	%	n	%	n	%	n	%
Q77	Survey instrument														
	I don't know	11	5.5	3	4.1	0	0.0	2	18.2	2	12.5	2	2.4	20	4.2
	No	39	19.6	14	19.2	14	18.0	2	18.2	3	18.8	18	22.0	97	20.5
	Yes	149	74.9	56	76.7	64	82.1	7	63.6	11	68.8	62	75.6	357	75.3
	Total	199	100.0	73	100.0	78	100.0	11	100.0	16	100.0	82	100.0	474	100.0
Q78	Type of survey instrument institution use to assess the first-year seminar? (Check all that apply)														
	I don't know	5	3.4	1	1.8	1	1.6	0	0.0	1	9.1	1	1.6	9	2.5
	A locally developed	120	80.5	50	89.3	53	82.8	7	100.0	10	90.9	55	88.7	300	84.0
	A national survey (e.g., NSSE, CCSSE, CIRP, EBI)	79	53.0	25	44.6	43	67.2	3	42.9	4	36.4	28	45.2	187	52.4
Q79	National survey was used: (Check all that apply)														
	Community College Survey of Student Engagement (CCSSE)	13	16.5	5	20.0	1	2.3	0	0.0	4	100.0	1	3.6	24	12.8
	Cooperative Institutional Research Program (CIRP) Freshman Survey	19	24.1	9	36.0	23	53.5	2	66.7	0	0.0	13	46.4	66	35.3

Item	Survey question	Extended orientation seminar		Academic seminar: uniform content		Academic seminar: various topics		Preprofessional or discipline-linked seminar		Basic study skills seminar		Hybrid		Total	
		n	%	n	%	n	%	n	%	n	%	n	%	n	%
Q79	National survey was used: Check all that apply (continued)														
	Cooperative Institutional Research Program (CIRP) Your First College Year (YFCY)	5	6.3	5	20.0	8	18.6	0	0.0	0	0.0	3	10.7	22	11.8
	First-Year Initiative (FYI)	8	10.1	2	8.0	3	7.0	0	0.0	1	25.0	2	7.1	18	9.6
	National Survey of Student Engagement (NSSE)	54	68.4	16	64.0	38	88.4	3	100.0	0	0.0	23	82.1	138	73.8
	Other (please specify)	20	25.3	3	12.0	11	25.6	0	0.0	1	25.0	3	10.7	39	20.9
Q81	Each outcome that was measured: (Check all that apply.)														
	Academic abilities	55	34.6	26	49.1	31	54.4	3	33.3	3	25.0	28	47.5	150	42.0
	Connections with peers	75	47.2	27	50.9	34	59.6	4	44.4	2	16.7	30	50.8	176	49.3
	Grade point average	92	57.9	32	60.4	29	50.9	5	55.6	6	50.0	40	67.8	207	58.0
	Out-of-class student/faculty interaction	72	45.3	20	37.7	34	59.6	4	44.4	3	25.0	29	49.2	168	47.1
	Participation in campus activities	81	50.9	27	50.9	22	38.6	6	66.7	3	25.0	32	54.2	175	49.0
	Persistence to graduation	63	39.6	26	49.1	17	29.8	2	22.2	4	33.3	25	42.4	137	38.4

Table continues p. 157

Table continued from p. 157

Item	Survey question	Extended orientation seminar		Academic seminar: uniform content		Academic seminar: various topics		Preprofessional or discipline-linked seminar		Basic study skills seminar		Hybrid		Total	
		n	%	*n*	%	*n*	%	*n*	%	*n*	%	*n*	%	*n*	%
Q81	Each outcome that was measured: Check all that apply *(continued)*														
	Persistence to sophomore year	121	76.1	39	73.6	40	70.2	6	66.7	5	41.7	47	79.7	263	73.7
	Satisfaction with faculty	101	63.5	42	79.2	51	89.5	6	66.7	6	66.6	40	67.8	253	70.9
	Satisfaction with the institution	101	63.5	41	77.4	38	66.7	7	77.8	4	33.3	36	61.0	233	65.3
	Use of campus services	96	60.4	25	47.2	22	38.6	7	77.8	1	8.3	26	44.1	182	51.0
	Other (please specify)	26	16.4	6	11.3	19	33.3	2	22.2	3	25.0	9	15.3	66	18.5
Q83	Release of data:														
	Please do not share my survey responses	144	41.9	51	37.5	44	35.2	15	50.0	22	55.0	51	38.9	342	41.0
	You may share my survey responses	200	58.1	85	62.5	81	64.8	15	50.0	18	45.0	80	61.1	493	59.0
	Total	344	100.0	136	100.0	125	100.0	30	100.0	40	100.0	131	100.0	835	100.0

Percentages may not sum to 100.0% due to rounding.

References

Barefoot, B. O. (1992). *Helping first-year college students climb the academic ladder: Report of a national survey of freshman seminar programming in American higher education* (Unpublished doctoral dissertation). College of William and Mary, Williamsburg, VA.

Barefoot, B. O., & Fidler, P. P. (1992). *The 1991 National Survey of Freshman Seminar Programs: Helping first-year college students climb the academic ladder* (Monograph No. 10). Columbia, SC, University of South Carolina, National Resource Center for The Freshman Year Experience and Students in Transition.

Barefoot, B. O., & Fidler, P. P. (1996). An historical and theoretical framework for the freshman seminar. In *The 1994 National Survey of Freshman Seminar Programs: Continuing innovations in the collegiate curriculum* (Monograph No. 20, pp. 5-9). Columbia, SC: University of South Carolina, National Resource Center for The Freshman Year Experience and Students in Transition.

Barefoot, B. O., Gardner, J. N., Cutright, M., Morris, L. V., Schroeder, C. C., Schwartz, S. W., Siegel, M. J., & Swing, R. L. (2005). *Achieving and sustaining institutional excellence for the first year of college*. San Francisco, CA: Jossey-Bass.

Brownell, J. E., & Swaner, L. E. (2010). *Five high-impact practices: Research on learning outcomes, completion, and quality*. Washington, DC: Association of American Colleges & Universities.

Caple, R. (1964). A rationale for the orientation course. *Journal of College Student Personnel, 6*, 42-46.

The Carnegie Foundation for the Advancement of Teaching. (n.d.). *Carnegie classification of institutions of higher education*. Retrieved from http://classifications.carnegiefoundation.org

Cohen, A. M., & Kisker, C. B. (2010). *The shaping of American higher education*. San Francisco, CA: Jossey-Bass.

Fitts, C. T., & Swift, F. H. (1928). The construction of orientation courses for college freshmen. *University of California Publications in Education, 1897-1929, 2*(3), 145-250.

Gahagan, J. S. (2002). A historical and theoretical framework for the first-year seminar. In *The 2000 National Survey of First-Year Seminar Programs: Continuing innovations in the collegiate curriculum* (Monograph No. 35, pp. 11-76). Columbia, SC: University of South Carolina, National Resource Center for The First-Year Experience and Students in Transition.

Gordon, V. N. (1989). Origins and purposes of the freshman seminar. In M. L. Upcraft, J. N. Gardner, & Associates, *The freshman year experience* (pp. 183-197). San Francisco, CA: Jossey-Bass.

Horn, L., Nunez, A. M., & Bobbitt, L. (2000). *Mapping the road to college: First-generation students' math track, planning strategies, and context of support* (NCES report 2000-153). Washington, DC: National Center for Education Statistics.

Huba, M. E., & Freed, J. E. (2000). *Learner-centered assessment on college campuses: Shifting the focus from teaching to learning*. Boston, MA: Allyn & Bacon.

Hunter, M. S., & Linder, C. W. (2005). First-year seminars. In M. L. Upcraft, J. N. Gardner, B. O. Barefoot, & Associates, *Challenging and supporting the first-year student: A handbook for improving the first year of college* (pp. 275-291). San Francisco, CA: Jossey-Bass.

Jewler, A. J. (1989). Elements of an effective seminar: The University 101 Program. In M. L. Upcraft, J. N. Gardner, & Associates, *The freshman year experience* (pp. 198-215). San Francisco, CA: Jossey-Bass.

Kaczmarek, P. G., Matlock, G., Merta, R., Ames, M. H., & Ross, M. (1994). An assessment of international college student adjustment. *International Journal for the Advancement of Counselling, 17*, 241-247.

Keup, J. R. (2005-2006). The impact of curricular interventions on intended second year re-enrollment. *Journal of College Student Retention: Research, Theory & Practice, 7*(1-2), 61-89.

Keup, J. R., & Petschauer, J. L. (2011). *The first-year seminar: Designing, implementing, and assessing courses to support student learning and success: Vol. I. Designing and administering the course.* Columbia, SC: University of South Carolina, National Resource Center for The First-Year Experience and Students in Transition.

Koch, A. K. (2001). *The first-year experience in American higher education: An annotated bibliography* (Monograph No. 3, 3rd ed.). Columbia, SC: University of South Carolina, National Resource Center for The First-Year Experience and Students in Transition.

Koch, A. K., Foote, S. M., Hinkle, S. E., Keup, J. R., & Pistilli, M. D. (2007). *The first-year experience in American higher education: An annotated bibliography* (Monograph No. 3, 4th ed.). Columbia, SC: University of South Carolina, National Resource Center for The First-Year Experience and Students in Transition.

Koch, A. K., & Gardner, J. N. (2006). The history of the first-year experience in the United States: Lessons from the past, practices in the present, and implications for the future. In A. Hamana & K. Tatsuo (Eds.), *The first-year experience and transition from high school to college: An international study of content and pedagogy.* Tokyo, Japan: Maruzen Publishing.

Leskes, A. & Miller, R. (2006). *Purposeful pathways: Helping students achieve key learning outcomes.* Washington, DC: Association of American Colleges & Universities.

Maki, P. (2004). *Assessing for learning: Building a sustainable commitment across the institution.* Sterling, VA: Stylus.

Markus, G. B., Howard, J. P. F., & King, D. C. (1993). Integrating community service and classroom instruction enhances learning: Results from an experiment. *Educational Evaluation and Policy Analysis, 15*(4), 410-419.

National Center for Education Statistics. (2010). *Integrated postsecondary education data system* [Data file]. Retrieved from http://nces.ed.gov/ipeds

Padgett, R. D., & Keup, J. R. (2010, November). *The impact of first-year seminars on college students' need for cognition.* Paper presented at the 35th Annual Meeting of the Association for the Study of Higher Education, Indianapolis, IN.

Pascarella, E. T., & Terenzini, P. T. (2005). *How college affects students, Vol. 2: A third decade of research.* San Francisco, CA: Jossey-Bass.

Pascarella, E. T., Cruce, T., Umbach, P. D., Wolniak, G. C., Kuh, G. D., Carini, R. M....Zhao, C-M. (2006). Institutional selectivity and good practices in undergraduate education: How strong is the link? *The Journal of Higher Education, 77*, 251-285.

Pascarella, E. T., Wolniak, G. C., Cruce, T. M., & Blaich, C. F. (2004). Do liberal arts colleges really foster good practices in undergraduate education? *Journal of College Student Development, 45*(1), 57-74.

Policy Center on the First Year of College. (2002). *2002 National Survey of First-Year Academic Practices findings.* Retrieved from http://www.jngi.org/2002nationalsurvey

Sandeen, A., & Barr, M. J. (2006). *Critical issues for student affairs: Challenges and opportunities.* San Francisco, CA: Jossey-Bass.

Saunders, D. F., & Romm, J. (2008). An historic perspective on first-year seminars. In B. F. Tobolowsky & Associates, *2006 National Survey of First-Year Seminars: Continuing innovations in the collegiate curriculum* (Monograph No. 51, pp. 1-4). Columbia, SC: University of South Carolina, National Resource Center for The First-Year Experience and Students in Transition.

Schuh, J. H. (2005). Assessing programs and other student experiences designed to enrich the first-year experience. In R. S. Feldman (Ed.), *Improving the first year of college: Research and practice* (pp. 141-157). Mahwah, NJ: Lawrence Erlbaum Associates.

Shanley, M. G., & Witten, G. H. (1990). University 101 freshman seminar: A longitudinal study of persistence, retention, and graduation rates. *NASPA Journal, 27*(4), 344-352.

Skipper, T. L., & Keup, J. R. (2010, March). *The 2009 National Survey on First-Year Seminars: Innovations in the undergraduate curriculum.* Presentation given at the 2010 ACPA Convention, Boston, MA.

Swing, R. L. (2001). *Proving and improving: Strategies for assessing the first college year* (Monograph No. 33). Columbia, SC: University of South Carolina, National Resource Center for The First-Year Experience and Students in Transition.

Terenzini, P. T., Springer, L., Yaeger, P. M., Pascarella, E. T., & Nora, A. (1996). First-generation college students: Characteristics, experiences, and cognitive development. *Research in Higher Education, 37*(1), 1-22.

Tinto, V. (1993). *Leaving college: Rethinking the causes and cures of student attrition* (2nd ed.). Chicago, IL: University of Chicago Press.

Tinto, V. (1998). Colleges as communities: Taking research on student persistence seriously. *The Review of Higher Education, 21*(2), 167-177.

Tobolowsky, B. F. (2005). *The 2003 National Survey on First-Year Seminars: Continuing innovations in the collegiate curriculum* (Monograph No. 41). Columbia, SC: University of South Carolina, National Resource Center for The First-Year Experience and Students in Transition.

Tobolowsky, B. F., & Associates. (2008). *2006 National Survey of First-Year Seminars: Continuing innovations in the collegiate curriculum* (Monograph No. 51). Columbia SC: University of South Carolina, National Resource Center for The First-Year Experience and Students in Transition.

Tobolowsky, B. F., Cox, B. E., & Wagner, M. T. (Eds.). (2005). *Exploring the evidence: Reporting research on first-year seminars, Volume III* (Monograph No. 42). Columbia SC: University of South Carolina, National Resource Center for The First-Year Experience and Students in Transition.

Upcraft, M. L. (2005). Assessing the first year of college. In M. L. Upcraft, J. N. Gardner, B. O. Barefoot, & Associates, *Challenging and supporting the first-year student: A handbook for improving the first year of college* (pp. 469-485). San Francisco, CA: Jossey-Bass.

Upcraft, M. L., Crissman Ishler, J. L., & Swing, R. L. (2005). A beginner's guide for assessing the first college year. In M. L. Upcraft, J. N. Gardner, B. O. Barefoot, & Associates, *Challenging and supporting the first-year student: A handbook for improving the first year of college* (pp. 486-500). San Francisco, CA: Jossey-Bass.

Upcraft, M. L., Gardner, J. N., & Associates. (1989). *The freshman year experience: Helping students survive and succeed in college.* San Francisco, CA: Jossey-Bass.

Upcraft, M. L., Gardner, J. N., Barefoot, B. O., & Associates. (2005). *Challenging and supporting the first-year student: A handbook for improving the first year of college.* San Francisco, CA: Jossey-Bass.

Zlotkowski, E. (Ed.). (2002). *Service-learning and the first-year experience: Preparing students for personal success and civic responsibility* (Monograph No. 34). Columbia, SC: University of South Carolina, National Resource Center for The First-Year Experience and Students in Transition.

Zlotkowski, E. (2005). Service-learning and the first-year student. In M. L. Upcraft, J. N. Gardner, B.O. Barefoot, & Associates (Eds.), *Challenging and supporting the first-year student* (pp. 256-370). San Francisco, CA: Jossey-Bass.

About the Authors

Ryan D. Padgett is the assistant director of research, grants, and assessment at the National Resource Center for The First-Year Experience and Students in Transition (NRC) at the University of South Carolina. In this role, Padgett coordinates all the research and assessment endeavors of the NRC. He facilitates a number of national surveys and oversees research collaborations and grant opportunities between the NRC and the higher education community and across the University of South Carolina campus. Before joining the NRC, Padgett was a research assistant at the Center for Research on Undergraduate Education at The University of Iowa and a project associate at the National Survey of Student Engagement (NSSE) at Indiana University. His research interests focus on students' transition from high school to college, particularly for underrepresented students; college choice and student access; transitional issues and college experiences for first-generation students; the impact of theoretical and vetted good practices, particularly during the first-year of college; and the effects of participation in high-impact practices.

Jennifer R. Keup is the director of the National Resource Center for The First-Year Experience and Students in Transition at the University of South Carolina where she provides leadership for the operational and strategic aspects of the Center. Before joining the staff of the National Resource Center, Keup had professional roles in the national dialogue on the first-year experience as well as higher education research and assessment as a project director at the Higher Education Research Institute (HERI) and was heavily involved in institutional assessment efforts as the director of the Student Affairs Information and Research Office (SAIRO) at the University of California-Los Angeles. Her research interests focus on students' personal and academic development during the transition from high school to college; the influence of campus programming on adjustment to college; and issues of institutional impact, responsiveness, and transformation in higher education.